PLANNING AND CONDUCTING AGENCY-BASED RESEARCH

FOURTH EDITION

Alex Westerfelt

Tracy J. Dietz
Texas Christian University

Allyn & Bacon

Boston   New York   San Francisco
Mexico City   Montreal   Toronto   London   Madrid   Munich   Paris
Hong Kong   Singapore   Tokyo   Cape Town   Sydney

Senior Acquisitions Editor: Patricia Quinlin
Editorial Assistant: Carly Czech
Senior Marketing Manager: Wendy Albert
Production Assistant: Maggie Brobeck
Manufacturing Buyer: Debbie Rossi
Cover Administrator: Joel Gendron

10 9 8 7 6 5 4 3 2 1   13 12 11 10 09

Allyn & Bacon
is an imprint of

www.pearsonhighered.com

ISBN-10:   0-205-63685-3
ISBN-13: 978-0-205-63685-3

ABOUT THE AUTHORS

ALEX WESTERFELT provides program design and evaluation consultation to foundations and community-based organizations. He has assisted federal, state, and community agencies in the areas of child welfare, Head Start, HIV prevention, homelessness, and public health. His practice experience is in child welfare, mental health, and public health where he has developed, delivered, and evaluated innovative social services. He has taught practice and research courses at undergraduate and graduate levels. Alex can be reached at alexwesterfelt@sbcglobal.net.

TRACY J. DIETZ is associate professor of social work at Texas Christian University where she teaches undergraduate research and field seminar. She is also a field faculty liaison. Her undergraduate students have planned and conducted agency-based research projects as part of their field education requirements for over 10 years. Her current interests are in developing, providing and evaluating support and services for Mexican-American cancer care-givers. Tracy can be reached at t.dietz@tcu.edu.

CONTENTS

Chapter 14
Data Analysis for Single-Case
Design Research   **163**

Chapter 15
Writing the Final Report   **167**

Bibliography   **173**

INTRODUCTION

In earlier editions of this workbook, we lamented social work students' lack of interest in research methods and, upon graduation, their failure to conduct research as part of their practice (Epstein, 1987; Kirk, 1990; Kirk & Fisher, 1976; Marino, Green, & Young, 1998). The current evidence-based practice movement in social work is, much to our delight, increasingly drawing practitioners to the published literature to identify best practices as they consider interventions for their work with clients. Moreover, we hope that evidence-based practice is changing social workers' attitudes about research overall and encouraging them to conduct meaningful agency-based research.

Coursework in research methods remains an essential component of social work education. Now, more than ever, students must have opportunities to apply research knowledge and skills outside the classroom—ideally in their field placement (Dietz, Westerfelt, & Barton, 2004)—in order to prepare them for careers which demand practice decisions based on empirical evidence.

The purpose of this workbook is to provide undergraduate and graduate social work faculty and students a systematic series of research assignments leading to a completed research study or proposal that students could carry out in their field placements. These assignments have four ultimate goals: (1) to increase students' interest and skills in practice research; (2) to help students produce agency-based research that contributes to the mission of the agency; (3) to demonstrate to students the value and utility of practice-based research; and (4) to create a new generation of social workers who understand and value, as well as contribute to, evidence-based practice. Our premise is that once students experience success in carrying out a research project in a practice setting and see the usefulness of their findings, they will have the confidence and motivation to continue research efforts in their own postgraduate practice.

Social work has long recognized the importance of field education as a means for integrating knowledge and practice skills. We believe that the field setting also provides students an ideal opportunity to apply research concepts and methods learned in research courses and to see firsthand how their research projects can benefit clients and agencies. For both student and practitioner, conducting research in the field can lead to an appreciation for the role of research in daily practice.

AGENCY-BASED RESEARCH

This workbook is designed to aid anyone who is planning and conducting research projects based in an agency setting. We define agency-based research as applied research with the goal of producing information that can be used to improve conditions and services for clients. This is in contrast to basic research, which seeks to generate theory or lead to a deeper understanding of an issue (i.e., knowledge for the sake of knowledge). Agency-based research involves studying some aspect of the agency and its programs or its clients and their communities with an emphasis on the utility of that information. Applied research should inform action, enhance decision making, and lead to solutions of human and societal problems (Patton, 1990).

ACKNOWLEDGMENTS

We would like to thank the following people for their suggestions for the fourth edition of the workbook: Melinda Pilkinton, Mississippi State University; Allen Rubin, University of Texas; and Sakinah Salahu-Din, Florida Gulf Coast University. We also thank our editor at Pearson, Patricia Quinlin, and her assistant, Carly Czech.

A NOTE FROM THE AUTHORS

We would like to hear about your experiences using the workbook. Your comments about what was most and least helpful will help us improve future editions. Please send your comments to us. Include the course for which the workbook was assigned and which sections of the workbook were unclear or difficult to complete. We look forward to hearing from you. Tracy J. Dietz, Ph.D., LMSW, TCU Department of Social Work, Texas Christian University, Box 298750, Fort Worth, Texas, 76129, or t.dietz@tcu.edu.

LAYOUT OF THE WORKBOOK

IF YOU WANT TO KNOW:	*TURN TO . . .*
✓ What research has the agency already completed? ✓ What data does the agency routinely collect?	**Chapter 1:** Orientation to Agency Research
✓ How do I develop a research question?	**Chapter 3:** The Research Question
✓ What has already been written about my topic and how do I find that information? ✓ How do I write a literature review?	**Chapter 4:** The Literature Review: Finding and Evaluating Practice-Based Information
✓ What is the best way to answer my research question?	**Chapter 5:** Choosing Your Methodology *See also:* **Chapter 6:** Survey Research **Chapter 7:** Qualitative Research **Chapter 8:** Single-Case Design **Chapter 9:** Outcome Evaluation
✓ How do I choose participants for my study? ✓ What sampling method should I use?	**Chapter 10:** Sample Design
✓ What procedures are necessary to safeguard research participants?	**Chapters 2 and 11:** Protection of Research Participants
✓ How do I analyze my findings and present my results?	**Chapter 12:** Data Analysis for Surveys and Outcome Evaluation **Chapter 13:** Data Analysis for Qualitative Research **Chapter 14:** Data Analysis for Single-Case Design Research
✓ How do I present my study?	**Chapter 15:** Writing the Final Report

HOW TO USE THIS WORKBOOK

To use this workbook effectively, students should either have completed a research methods course or currently be enrolled in one. Although the workbook is designed to follow the basic steps of the research process as covered by any research methods text, it is not a research textbook and will not present foundation material. Rather, it asks questions students must answer as they plan and conduct a research study. We intend that the workbook be used in conjunction with a research text, and throughout the workbook we remind students to draw upon their text.

The workbook is designed to guide students in the completion of an agency-based project within either a one or two-semester research sequence. The Timeline on page 56 provides a list of the tasks to be completed and the estimated time to be allotted to each one. We encourage students to use this for planning purposes.

The workbook provides guidelines for the development of four methods commonly used in agency-based research:

- Survey research
- Qualitative research
- Single-case design research
- Program outcome evaluation.

For each method, we outline the steps we think necessary for completing a research study utilizing that method. We recognize that the steps laid out in this workbook may differ from those presented in other texts, but we expect that the differences will be slight. Further, we recognize that there are many acceptable ways of conducting research.

For each step of the research process we detail what students should include when writing that section of the research paper. We recommend that students use the workbook pages to make notes as they compile their beginning thoughts and ideas. Then, develop initial drafts at the computer, using the outline numbering of each workbook chapter for consistency and structure in composing sections of the paper. The advantages of this option are to provide the instructor with typed copy, and once the instructor provides feedback, to allow students to incorporate it into their draft documents more easily. By the time the students have completed the workbook, they will have a substantial draft of their paper.

Because the terms *field instructor*, *field supervisor*, and *field liaison* are often used interchangeably, we want to clarify the terms we use. In the workbook *field instructor* is used to refer to the agency staff member who is responsible for supervising the student. *Course instructor* refers to the university faculty member who is teaching the course in which the workbook is being used. *Field liaisons* are typically university faculty members whose role is to coordinate the students' learning experiences in both the agency and the university. A program may give different responsibilities to different individuals; for example, a program may provide a significant role for a field liaison in the research project. When there are variations from the definitions or names given here, it would be helpful to designate for students the individuals who correspond to the course instructor and the field instructor as identified in the workbook.

NOTE TO STUDENTS

Regardless of whether you are a BSW, MSW, or Ph.D. student, we believe you will find this book to be a valuable resource in designing and completing an agency-based research project. We recommend while using the workbook to guide your research project, you make a habit of referring to both your research text and the suggested articles for the particular method of study you choose. In the Table of Contents you will see the four methods listed. At the beginning of each of the chapters we have indicated a specific article or articles that will provide you with an example of a research study that utilizes that method. Reference to your methods text is intended for review of material; reference to the article will give you a complete picture of an actual study and an example of how to write sections of your own study.

Keep in mind that the research process is an ongoing feedback loop. As explained, it may appear quite linear, but in actuality, research activities may not follow the orderly steps we present. Inevitably, you will find yourself returning to prior steps to revise them based on what you have found in later steps. Eventually the pieces of the puzzle will all fit together. Trust us.

We have designed the workbook in an easy-to-follow, step-by-step format that we believe demystifies the research process. We hope it will build your confidence in your ability to participate in and conduct research in an agency setting. Please refer to page 56 for an outline of the research steps, tasks, and time estimates. This should help you in breaking down the larger task of a research project into manageable pieces and planning your time accordingly.

NOTE TO COURSE INSTRUCTORS

The workbook can be used in a variety of courses. It is an obvious addition to a research course, but we intentionally designed it for use in a field seminar or a practice course that is taken concurrently with field activity. We encourage faculty to experiment with various options for coverage of this material. The following social work program components are considerations for determining the ideal format: research course requirements and expectations, block versus concurrent placements, the proximity of placements to each other, the primary instructor, and the other people involved in guiding the student project.

We include a suggested timeline for you on page 56 based on a 15-week, one semester course and for a 30-week, two semester course. The timelines are intended to help you structure the workbook chapters and assignments to best fit with the time available for your students' projects as well as to help students in breaking down the research tasks and developing a realistic timeline for completion.

Some course instructors, faced with certain program constraints, may want students to complete only a research proposal and not actually carry out the project. Others may want students to work in groups and complete group research projects. In large programs where individual agencies may have several students in placement, students could work together on one project for the agency. One reviewer of an earlier edition whose program used a one semester block placement told us that she asked her field instructors to develop research questions for their students. The students were given their research questions the first week and started immediately on their projects.

A computer template is available to course instructors who adopt the workbook. The purpose of the template is to enable students to more readily move their thoughts and ideas from the pages of the workbook to a computer. We hope that this aid will help students as they organize and write the first drafts of their papers. Once the first draft is on computer, revisions should be much easier for students. Further, course instructors may find typed drafts of the workbook assignments easier to read and evaluate. The template includes the section headings and questions of the workbook assignments and may be used with your students. If you are interested in obtaining the template, you may contact Tracy Dietz at t.dietz@tcu.edu.

NOTE TO FIELD INSTRUCTORS

You are a key player in your students' research projects. Your view of research and the value you place on it will affect their experiences with agency research. However, you will not be totally responsible for helping them conduct the research project. The course instructor is responsible for teaching the students basic research methods and the application of these to agency settings.

Your role is to support and monitor the students along the way. You will be able to provide the best assistance if you are involved from the beginning. The steps we outline in the workbook promote your involvement by requiring students to ask questions of you and other agency staff. Your comments and feedback to them are necessary and will be extremely helpful.

You are an expert about your agency and its clients. You know what questions, when answered, will provide information that will benefit the clients. You may also be an expert in conducting research. However, you do not need a strong research background to work with students. If you lack confidence in your ability to help them with research projects, this workbook will serve as a resource to you as well.

Research resources for field instructors are available from faculty members. You could request that your school presents a seminar for field instructors that focuses on conducting agency research. In addition, we provide a bibliography at the end of the workbook for more information on conducting agency-based research.

NOTE TO PRACTITIONERS

This workbook can help practitioners fulfill their commitment to research. Whether developing an evaluation plan as part of a grant proposal or conducting a research project, agency staff will find the workbook a valuable step-by-step resource. For agency use, we recommend starting with Chapter 3 to clarify the research question and then continuing with the following chapters of the workbook.

CHAPTER 1

ORIENTATION TO AGENCY RESEARCH

Two major arguments support the need for incorporating a research perspective into one's practice. First, our professional code of ethics emphasizes the responsibility of social workers to understand, utilize, and conduct research. Accordingly, professional responsibility requires that we draw on and contribute to the knowledge base of social work.

Second, we are accountable to those we seek to assist. We are responsible for knowing the struggles, needs, and assets of those we assist and for providing the services that make a difference. Only through our continuous search for better understanding and the testing of current understanding can we effectively assist others.

As part of the curriculum in your social work program, you have been exposed to various aspects of research. Much of the information you have acquired is the result of others' research endeavors. In addition, you have either taken a specific research methods class or are currently enrolled in one. Now you are ready to move beyond the role of consumer of research to that of producer of research by conducting a research project at your field placement.

The best way to begin this process is by familiarizing yourself with the research efforts that have already been undertaken at your agency. To that end, we provide the following questions for you to consider as you begin your research project.

For students in social work field placements, start by talking with your field instructor and proceed to individuals he or she recommends. Often agency staff can help you understand the agency's own research program. You may need to ask more than one person to get a clear picture.

If the agency has a research program, complete the questions in Section A. If the agency does not have a research program, complete the questions in Section B.

A. IF THE AGENCY HAS A RESEARCH PROGRAM

1) What are its goals and purposes?

2) Who is responsible for overseeing agency research? Interview that person, and ask whether the research is done in-house or contracted out. If in-house, what is the size of the research budget? How many staff members are involved in research activities? If done by contract, how often have studies been done in the past and by whom?

3) What resistance, if any, from staff and/or clients has been encountered in agency research efforts?

4) How and to whom does the agency distribute its research findings?

5) How have staff members used the findings?

6) What changes at the agency have resulted from research findings?

7) What is the agency process for obtaining permission to conduct a research study? (If there is no agency process in place, we encourage you to obtain written permission to carry out your study from the director of the agency. The procedures for study approval and protecting human subjects are discussed in Chapters 2 and 11.)

8) What studies or reports have been done at the agency? Obtain copies of two recent reports, indicate the purpose of each, and write a short summary paragraph for each report.

Now, go to Section C.

B. IF THE AGENCY DOES NOT HAVE A RESEARCH PROGRAM

1) Find out what information the agency collects for annual reports, funding reports, or community public relations. This may involve the number and characteristics of service recipients, needs assessments, or client satisfaction studies. What information has the agency collected? If there have been no data collection efforts, explore why that is.

2) How and by whom is the collected information used?

3) How and to whom does the agency distribute this information? How have staff members used the information?

4) What changes at the agency have resulted from the information?

5) What is the agency process for obtaining permission to conduct a research study? (If there is no agency process in place, we encourage you to obtain written permission to carry out your study from the director of the agency. The procedures for study approval and protecting human subjects are discussed in Chapters 2 and 11.)

6) What reports have been done at the agency? Obtain copies of two recent reports, indicate the purpose of each, and write a short summary paragraph for each report.

C.   STAFF VIEWS AND USAGE OF RESEARCH

Interview two staff members, one of whom should be your field instructor.

    1) How do they view research? Summarize their responses.

    2) How do they use research to improve practice?

3) What research-oriented journals or books are frequently used by them? How often do they read these journals?

4) How have they used information from a specific journal article in the past month?

D. AGENCY RESOURCES FOR YOUR RESEARCH

What are the agency resources that will be available to you as you conduct your research project? Indicate what you find out about staff assistance (e.g., clerical and computer), photocopying, mail, computer access, and anything else that may be relevant to your project.

E. TIMELINE FOR YOUR RESEARCH PROJECT

Planning and conducting an agency-based research project can be overwhelming even for seasoned practitioners. It is a daunting task to complete a project as part of a one-semester course, so planning ahead is essential. We recommend that you take a few moments now and review the remainder of the workbook to see what lies ahead.

Pay special attention to the Timeline found on page 56 for completing your project. It is important to develop a timeline, working backwards from a projected completion date. A research project involves many steps with multiple tasks. Often your work will not progress in a step-wise fashion. You will be working on several steps at the same time and returning to work that you previously thought completed. Finally, allow time for delays and expect the unexpected. As Murphy supposedly once said, if something can go wrong, it will. We think Murphy was a social work researcher.

CHAPTER 2

PROTECTION OF RESEARCH PARTICIPANTS (PRELIMINARY)

We have included two chapters on the protection of research participants. We want you to consider safeguards for participants from the initial conception of your study through its completion. We find that students (and even seasoned researchers) are in a better position to prepare applications for review of participant safeguards and study procedures once they have designed their study. However, time constraints may require you to submit materials *before* the study is completely designed. Consequently, we introduce the process early on so that you can explore university and agency requirements. Then, in Chapter 11 we guide you through the basic requirements for protection of research participants.

Protection of the people who participate in a research study is a primary responsibility of the researcher. This obligation is generally fulfilled through the use of a consent form and through the early peer review of the researcher's study via submission of the proposed study to a review committee. These review committees are typically called Institutional Review Boards (IRBs), but some universities may have another name for their review committee, for example, Human Subjects Review committee. Agencies may or may not have research review committees as well. The responsibility of the IRB is to review all research involving "human subjects." We prefer the term *research participants* in keeping with our emphasis on the participation and contribution of clients in the research process. You cannot proceed with data collection until you have approval from the IRB.

Federal regulations provide the basis for IRB procedures and the actual evaluation of study safeguards, but the regulations leave room for varying interpretation. Thus, our discussion is necessarily general rather than specific, and the exercises that follow will direct you in learning more about your specific IRB.

An excellent on-line resource for more information about the protection of human subjects can be found at the U.S. Department of Health and Social Services, http://www.hhs.gov/ohrp/policy/. Your university's research office may have a web page or other information that will guide you in preparing your application for Human Subjects Review. The National Institutes of Health's (NIH) Office of Human Subjects Research has developed online training: "Protecting Human Research Participants," which can be used to fulfill the obligation for education in the area of human participant protection. Their web address is: http://phrp.nihtraining.com/users/login.php. The tutorial presents information related to protection of human participants, and includes text, case studies, and exercises to help researchers learn the basics of human subjects protection.

You must submit your study design for review *before* you begin collecting data. Some IRBs require that you submit a certificate of completion of the on-line training mentioned above with your application. Some IRBs have strict timeframes for review of and response to submissions. As noted above, this may necessitate a submission from you *before* you have had time to complete the necessary sections of this workbook and develop your study design. In that case, you need to work closely with your course instructor to meet the IRB requirements.

Keep in mind that it is *not* the function of these committees to evaluate your study design and methods, but rather to evaluate the extent to which you will protect research participants from any harm. This includes physical, social, psychological, and legal harm.

For example, if you are studying people recently paroled from prison, how will you make sure they do not feel any coercion to participate in your study? What if they mistakenly believe that their parole officer *expects* them to participate? For some studies you must address how you will handle information you receive that involves illegal behaviors. You will always have to discuss how you will keep information confidential.

Consider what is needed if your study involves sensitive information. For example, if you ask information about a past sexual assault and a person becomes emotionally upset, what are your plans to handle that type of situation? As part of your application for IRB approval, you must describe all potential risks involved in your study and the procedures for protecting against or minimizing those risks, including risks to confidentiality.

A word about online surveys: Specific IRB requirements for collecting data electronically may vary from university to university. Prior to preparing your human subjects review application for administering an online survey, contact your IRB committee to find out the specific procedures that they require.

REMINDER:
Build enough time into your study's timetable to allow the IRB to review your application.

A.   THE UNIVERSITY IRB

Students conducting research projects as part of their educational requirements must submit an application for human subjects' protections with their university IRB. Find out the name of the university IRB and contact its chairperson or director regarding application for approval of your study's procedures. Obtain a copy of the application packet to review and begin preparing. Be sure to ask about the time frames for submission of applications and the expected date for response.

Indicate with whom you talked and what information you received.

B.   THE AGENCY IRB

Find out the agency's procedure for the review and approval of research studies. Ask for a copy of the procedures for submission. Also ask about the time frames for submission of applications and the expected date for response.

If the agency has no formalized procedures, we strongly encourage you to submit to the agency your University IRB application, and obtain, in writing, the agency director's permission to carry out your study.

Indicate the names of those with whom you talked and what information you received.

C. PREPARE A TIMELINE FOR YOUR HUMAN SUBJECTS' REVIEW APPLICATION

If you need to submit your application for approval of study procedures very soon, consult the IRB guidelines and turn to Chapter 11 to prepare your application.

TASKS	DATES
Draft of IRB application due to your course instructor *Receive comments from your course instructor and make corrections based on instructor feedback.*	_____
IRB application due to University IRB committee*	_____
Agency application due	_____
IRB notification on your application expected* *Once application is approved, data collection can begin. Keep in mind that you may have to make revisions and resubmit.*	_____
If applicable, resubmission due	_____
If applicable, final IRB approval expected	_____

***After course instructor approval, add the starred dates to your study timeline on page x.**

CHAPTER 3

THE RESEARCH QUESTION

REMINDER:
   Review the section of your research text regarding formation of the research question, problem, or topic.

In this chapter you will develop your initial research question. We say "initial" because oftentimes as people begin looking at articles related to their topic of interest, they learn more about the topic or about ways it has been studied that help them reshape their research question. We want to help you brainstorm possible questions of interest to you. Developing a clear research question is crucial to help you stay focused as you complete the other steps of the study. We encourage students, once they have finalized their research questions, to write it inside the cover of the workbook or somewhere prominent in their notebooks. Referring to it as you review the literature will help you avoid veering off on a tangent or feeling overwhelmed.

Keep in mind that a research question is not the same as a hypothesis. A hypothesis is your expectation about how events or phenomena will be related *based on some prior study and understanding of the events or phenomena.* A research question is just that, a question. It asks exactly what you would like to know, *not* what is already known or what can be expected. For example, "What is the impact of chronic illness on children's coping skills?" is a research question. A hypothesis is a statement. "Children living with chronic illness will have fewer coping skills than children who are not chronically ill" is a hypothesis.

Social workers assess client strengths and successes as readily as they assess problems and needs. As you think about possible questions for your study, consider research questions that seek to learn not only about problems and needs but also about strengths and successes. Be as interested in "what is going right" as in "what is going wrong."

Discovering how people survive stressful situations and crises can contribute valuable information to the profession as it develops programs and services. Uncovering the strengths of certain types of families or communities can enhance workers' practice knowledge. Encouraging people to tell their stories in their own words not only recognizes that they have something to offer but also reminds us that research, like practice, can benefit from a cooperative, interactive approach.

Answering each of the questions in this chapter will guide you in developing your research question. As ideas come to mind, put them in question form.

A WORD ABOUT EVIDENCE-BASED PRACTICE

If you're considering a research question about the effectiveness of a particular program or intervention at the agency, or your effectiveness with one client or a group of clients, you have stepped into the realm of evidence-based practice. Evidence-based practice is essentially a reflective approach to working with others.

When I do X with clients, does it help? How do I know it helps? Is that my definition or theirs or both? Does it help some, but not others? Why does it help? Or not help? What are others finding? Would something else be more helpful or be more cost effective but no less effective?

Evidence-based practice requires critical thinking skills and intentionality. The best practitioners are always questioning and examining not only their own work but also whatever is being promoted in their sphere of practice as the next best thing. When everyone is talking about X, the critical thinking practitioners are asking about the *evidence* for X.

An evidence-based practice approach is an easy concept to understand. It's smart consumer as smart practitioner. When smart consumers make purchases—e.g., a mattress, computer, car—they research and find out what the evidence is relative to the criteria they deem important to their decision—quality, reliability, cost. Smart consumers can even examine empirical evidence for alternative health care claims and treatments at websites like the government's National Center for Complementary and Alternative Medicine, "dedicated to exploring complementary and alternative medical (CAM) practices in the context of rigorous science; training CAM researchers and disseminating authoritative information" (http://nccam.nih.gov/). Should we expect any less effort on the part of smart practitioners? When practitioners choose interventions or practice models, they should do so based on the available evidence.

What is hard to understand is why more consumers *don't* gather the evidence before they try or buy—which has its parallel in practice: why don't more practitioners gather evidence about an intervention before they try it or "buy" it? Why don't more practitioners generate evidence about the intervention they are already using?

Others (supervisor, colleague, workshop leader) may say that they know an intervention is effective based on others who have used it, something they read, or the fact that it's been called a best practice. In that case the smart practitioner asks for the documentation to check it out herself or himself.

The willingness to gather and assess evidence is what helps make a good practitioner better. Historically, it was much more difficult to gather evidence, and people relied primarily on workshops, a few journals they might subscribe to, and practice wisdom. Now, however, practitioners have access to many journals online as well as websites narrowly focused on particular practice areas. For example, the Centers for Disease Control and Prevention (CDC) has an entire section devoted to "interventions represent[ing] the strongest HIV behavioral interventions in the literature to date that have been rigorously evaluated and have demonstrated efficacy in reducing HIV or STD incidence or HIV-related risk behaviors or promoting safer behaviors." Check out: http://www.cdc.gov/hiv/topics/research/prs/evidence-based-interventions.htm

In only a few hours it's now possible to gather information about many interventions targeting individuals, families, groups, and communities, as well as efforts in the policy arena. Granted, some of you may have launched an Internet search, and, overwhelmed by the 3,425,292 search results returned, closed the window. That's why we encourage people to prepare for a search by starting with others who know the territory and with search engines that narrow the results (for example, Google Scholar). We discuss this in more depth in the next chapter, but for now we encourage you to begin there or with people in the field or the university who could quickly get you started searching the literature.

A word of caution: It's easy to move from taking someone's word that an intervention works to taking someone's word that it is a best practice. Increasingly, practitioners are being pressured to adopt "best practices." But simply because an intervention is labeled a best or evidence-based practice, as in the CDC example above, does not absolve you of the responsibility to be a critical thinker and determine if it's the best practice for your clients.

Consider with whom the intervention was tested. Is that your population? How is your population similar or different? Have the measurement instruments been validated with your population? Are they culturally appropriate? Are the methods feasible in your setting? What adjustments might be necessary? Do you need special training in using the methods in the study or administering the measurement instruments? Would the intervention be acceptable to your clients? Even if you choose to use a particular evidence-based intervention, you still have a responsibility to examine its effectiveness with your clients.

Reflective, empirically-based practice is difficult. There are never enough resources or time to explore and consider all the options. The context in which one intervenes can be chaotic and unpredictable. People drop out of treatment, groups fail to coalesce, some participants don't complete instruments, and agency staff members resign. That's okay—it's the journey not the destination that's important. Don't lose track of the primary goal: reflective practice.

Back to your research question. For those of you considering a question on practice effectiveness, bear in mind that how to *implement* an intervention is a different question from how *effective* an intervention is. For the purposes of an outcome evaluation, you want to focus on the latter. You may not know what interventions have been applied to the issue or population you want to study. In that case your first trip to the library or to consult with a professional may be to find what's been done relative to this issue and what's being done currently at your agency.

In the end, for a research question about practice effectiveness, you want a research question that includes the targeted ***population*** (e.g., criminal offenders on probation with substance abuse diagnoses), ***intervention(s)*** (e.g., cognitive behavioral therapy alone versus cognitive behavioral therapy combined with medication), and intended *result(s)* (e.g., completion of probation without re-offending).

Make notes on your initial ideas for a research question.

A.   WHAT WOULD YOU LIKE TO KNOW?

✓ Perhaps you are interested in knowing more ***about the clients*** who are served by the agency:
   —their characteristics, including strengths and needs
   —their satisfaction with the agency's services
   —their experiences—with obstacles they face either in daily living or in accessing services
   —their experiences with agency services or the lack of services

✓ Perhaps you are interested in knowing more ***about the workers*** at the agency:
   —their practice orientation
   —their job satisfaction

✓ Perhaps you are interested in knowing more ***about the services*** at the agency:
   —the extent to which services address the needs of people in the community
   —the extent to which they reach the target population
   —their impact or effectiveness (outcomes)

Which of the above are you interested in exploring?

B. WHAT WOULD THE AGENCY LIKE TO KNOW?

1) Talk to your field instructor or anyone else at the agency she or he recommends as a good source of information for this question. Jot down their ideas for research they think would be of value to the agency. Be open to all their ideas and begin thinking of possible research questions that might blend their interests with yours.

Indicate first names of people to whom you spoke and their position in the agency. What topics are they interested in? Put their ideas into questions.

2) Present your ideas to them for your research question. Indicate their feedback.

C.   WHAT WOULD THE CLIENTS LIKE TO KNOW?

Check with your field instructor about talking to some of the clients with whom you have contact. If you don't yet have contact, ask your field instructor to recommend to you some clients with whom you could talk about this.

Our students' experiences have been that using the word "research" can be as confusing to clients as to students. So, we recommend that you avoid using the word "research" when talking with them. Assessment is a good alternative. Or, tell clients that, as a student, you are interested in gathering information that would be helpful to the agency. Ask them what topics they think might be helpful for the agency to know more about.

Indicate the first names or initials of people to whom you spoke. What topics would they be interested in learning more about? Put their ideas into questions.

D.   WHAT IS YOUR RESEARCH QUESTION?

On the next page we provide some research questions that our students have investigated, organized by the type of study they designed. Look them over for ideas about your own question.

Now take your first stab at coming up with a research question. Based on your thinking, interests, and discussions with others, write out one or two questions you would be interested in pursuing.

LIST OF STUDENT RESEARCH QUESTIONS AND DESIGN TYPE

SURVEY RESEARCH

- What Is the Employee Turnover and Job Satisfaction in the Field of Disabilities?
- What Is Foster Parent Satisfaction of Case Management Services Provided by Private Versus Public Agencies?
- How Does Attitudinal Change Relate to Length of Stay for Substance Abusers in Treatment?
- What Are the Characteristics of Programs in Public Administration Offices for Court-Appointed Guardians?
- What Are the Characteristics of Juvenile Offender Recidivists?
- What Are the Needs of Jewish Elders?

QUALITATIVE RESEARCH

- How Do Nurse Case Managers and Social Worker Case Managers Describe Case Management Roles?
- What Are the Ethical Restrictions on Dual Relationships among Different Mental Health Professions?
- What Are the Factors Leading to Relapse in Women Who Are Chemically Addicted?
- What Are the Experiences of Clients with Severe and Persistent Mental Illness Who Are in Community Corrections?

SINGLE-CASE DESIGN

- What Is the Effect of Classroom Reinforcement on Classroom Behavior Change?
- What Is the Effect of Physical Exercise on an Alzheimer's Patient's Aggressive Behavior toward Others?

OUTCOME EVALUATION

- How Does Staff Training Improve Staff Knowledge about Sexuality for People with Disabilities?
- How Effective Is a Cultural Consciousness-Raising Group on Empowerment of Latino Women?
- How Effective Is an Anger Management Group on Skill Development of Sixth Graders?
- How Effective Is an Educational Support Group for Hepatitis C Patients?

E. BROWSE THE LITERATURE RELATED TO YOUR TOPIC

Now make a quick trip to the library or search an online database such as Google Scholar or others listed in Chapter 4 just to see what information is available on your topic. This is *not* the time to do a thorough literature review; that will come later. For now, simply see if there are several current articles on your topic and choose two (preferably from social work journals). Don't hesitate to ask reference librarians for help.

Skimming over these articles will give you an idea of the scope of the topic you have chosen and may help you in narrowing down your question. Our experience is that many students significantly change their question based on this first view of the literature. If, in the middle of this step—or the next one—you become less than enthusiastic about your research question, do not hesitate to abandon it and pursue another.

For now, list the author, title, and reference information for two articles you examined and a two- or three-sentence summary of each.

    1) Author and Date:
       Title:
       Citation Information:
       Summary:

    2) Author and Date:
       Title:
       Citation Information:
       Summary:

F.   REFINE YOUR RESEARCH QUESTION

Refine your research question based on your literature review using the following checklist:

✓ Is the research question relevant to social work? How does the issue involve social work?

✓ What makes this issue or problem significant? What is the scope of the issue? (Who is affected? How many people are affected? In what ways?)

✓ By answering your question, how could the information impact services to clients at your agency or improve practice?

✓ If a question is about effectiveness of services, does it include the targeted population, intervention(s), and intended result(s)?

✓ Is a study to answer your question feasible? In other words, can you reasonably do what is necessary to answer your research question? Address this relative to the time you have been given to do the study, money that is available for expenses of the study (e.g., photocopying and mailing), ethical and logistical considerations, the amount of assistance you will need from others (interviewers, computer consultation, practice consultation, data analysis), and the amount of cooperation you will need from agency personnel. Be realistic in your estimations because it may help you focus a research question that is too ambitious.

✓ Which research method will you use? Begin to think about the best way (research method) to answer your question. Would qualitative or quantitative methods be most appropriate? (Don't hesitate to return to your methods text for a quick review of these approaches.) This workbook offers guidance on four methods of research: survey, qualitative, single-case design, and outcome evaluation. Which method do you think would provide the best information to answer your question? Why?

G. FINALIZE YOUR RESEARCH QUESTION

Share your research question with your peers and field instructor, soliciting their feedback.

Indicate first names of people you asked for feedback and what questions or suggestions they had.

Write your revised research question below:

CHAPTER 4

THE LITERATURE REVIEW: FINDING AND EVALUATING PRACTICE-BASED INFORMATION

One of the main purposes of conducting a literature review is to help you become more knowledgeable about your research topic. Keep in mind that a literature review is both a process and a product. The process of conducting a literature review helps you learn more about your topic and provides guidance on how to carry out your own study. You will conduct a better study if you know what other people have said about your topic, how they designed their studies, and what they have found in their own studies. The product of conducting a literature review is a written review that explains the importance and relevance of your topic based on what has already been written and shows how your study will add to what is already known.

Quantitative methods typically involve a deductive approach to research. Thus, you begin by reviewing the literature to develop your ideas regarding what information to collect in your study. In *qualitative* research, there is a debate about when to review the literature. Some proponents of qualitative research suggest doing the literature review later in the study. According to this view, your research will be "pure" in the sense that it will not be guided or biased—perhaps in a wrong direction—by what is known about your topic and what has been done by other researchers. Other qualitative researchers value the early review of literature to better understand the topic and to design the best possible study.

We believe that reviewing the literature first is essential, and we guide you in completing that step before you proceed with the other steps of conducting either a quantitative or qualitative study. This way you can compare your plans for your study to what others have done with an eye for improving your project. A literature review can keep you from "reinventing the wheel" by suggesting ways to conceptualize (define) the question and operationalize (measure) the variables. The literature will also help you identify existing measurement instruments. While a considerable part of the literature review is conducted early, remember to think of the literature review as an ongoing process. As your project unfolds and new questions arise, you will return to the literature for answers.

We assume you have access to a college library or the internet and computerized databases of abstracts and indexes relevant to social work, and that you are able (or will learn) to use them. Before sitting down at the keyboard, review and write down your research question. As you examine articles, keep your question in front of yourself to stay focused. This is a simple step that will help you stay on track.

Electronic searching is powerful and fast, but you can easily overdo it by locating literature that is, at best, peripheral to your topic. Before you start to search the literature, learn how to search effectively, how to do an advanced search, and how to expand or narrow your search, using Boolean operators, truncated terms or wildcards, and other features of electronic databases. Reference librarians are a tremendous help and we strongly urge you to work with them.

We have included at the end of this chapter a list of electronic databases commonly used in social work to assist you in your literature search. We encourage you to review the list and select those databases relevant to your topic.

We recommend that you keep a log of where and how you have searched the literature. If you later need assistance from a reference librarian or your instructor, you will be able to show them what you have already tried. The process of recording what you have done will also help you learn effective searching strategies.

Given the increasing availability of web-based information, it is critical to carefully evaluate the sources you will use in your study. In general, published articles in professional journals have undergone a peer review process in which manuscripts are reviewed by authorities in that area of research before being accepted for publication. This is not the case for many web-based sources. Web sources can provide factual information, promote opinions or viewpoints, or present inaccurate information.

Many university libraries provide guidelines or criteria for evaluating web-based sources. At a minimum, you should consider:

- Who is the author? What are his or her qualifications and credentials? Is this person a reputable source on the topic?
- Is the information accurate? Are references and links to related sites given? If the site does not present original data, from where did the information come? Is the source cited? In general, use actual research studies, not reports about a study that can misrepresent the author's intended meaning. Watch for errors in web sources. Grammatical and typographical errors should lead you to question the validity of the information on the site.
- Is the information current? What is the date on the site? When was it last revised?
- Is the information objective? Who sponsors the site? Avoid sources that offer opinions, attempt to persuade you, or sell products.
- Does the source provide comprehensive information? Is there depth and detail as well as breadth about the topic? Are reputable links given?

Evaluate all literature, including that published in quality journals, for its reliability, validity, and limitations. All studies have limitations and they are usually presented and discussed by the authors. Assess the impact of the limitations on the study's findings. These are ways you become a critical reader of research literature.

You should include a minimum of 10 references, no less than four empirical articles (actual studies with sample, methods, and findings), and at least six other scholarly references. The dates of publication of articles should be within the past five years. There are some exceptions to this—for example, a "classic" work that was written many years ago. Also, in a few cases you may find that your topic has been studied less often and requires a search beyond the past five years.

HELPFUL TIPS:

✓ Students often have difficulty determining whether an article is empirical or not. An empirical article is based on the results of an actual study that was designed and completed by the authors. *Empirical articles will be your most valuable resources when designing your study.* The authors provide information about the people who were in their sample, how the data were collected, and the findings. With few exceptions, the article will contain tables of data or, in the case of qualitative studies, excerpts from participant interviews. We recommend that you locate at least four articles that present as much information as possible about the design and execution of a research study. They will provide examples to assist you in designing your study.

✓ Some articles will report findings from other studies. These are *not* empirical articles as they usually do not contain information about how the study was conducted. However, the articles will include the source of the empirical articles they cite.

✓ "I can't find anything on my topic. There have been no studies done on this at all." This is the most common difficulty reported by students doing a literature review. Yes, often students cannot find anything; but it is seldom true that no work has been done on the topic. What we frequently find is that either the student has not sought the assistance of reference librarians who can help tailor a search of the literature, or the student is too narrowly restricting the search. For example, if the research question is to determine the needs of a community of First Nations people for their local service center, there may be no other published needs assessment of that group. However, you can probably find published studies of the needs of First Nations people in general— for example, surveys regularly conducted by the Indian Health Service. Also, you can locate articles that detail needs assessments done among other ethnic groups. Such articles, while not addressing your target group, will provide you with information on how to conduct a needs assessment with an identified group of individuals.

✓ Don't just use abstracts. Abstracts are brief summaries that should help you determine the relevance of the article to your work, but should not be used as a main source. If you must use abstracts because you are unable to access the full article, note that the information you are citing comes from the abstract.

✓ We encourage students to focus their efforts on identifying articles rather than books because articles are easier to digest. One exception is an edited book that often contains, in essence, a series of articles on a particular topic. Books that are complete reports of a single study or a series of studies can also be helpful. Dissertations completed by persons outside your own university can be difficult to obtain in a timely fashion. (They are sometimes identified in search results simply with the designation, Ph.D. or D.S.W.)

✓ You will think you have hit the mother lode if you find an article or book that is a current review of the literature, review of recent empirical work, compendium of best practices, or meta-analysis (meta as in comprehensive) of research studies relevant to your topic. Be sure it is relatively recent and, if narrowly focused in its choice of studies (either by population or intervention), be sure to continue searching for additional studies.

✓ You will find one of the best sources for references at the end of each article. All articles and books will list their references, and once you have identified a relevant work, its bibliography will provide you with several other sources of material. This is why finding the most recent literature is important. Authors are able to cite only works prior to their own.

✓ Keep in mind the overall purpose of conducting a literature review as you browse the literature. You should look for articles that:

   ▪ Introduce and provide a background for your topic
   ▪ Establish the importance of your topic
   ▪ Provide a theoretical basis for your study
   ▪ Address a client issue similar to yours
   ▪ Identify and measure variables used in prior studies
   ▪ Identify measurement instruments and methods of study
   ▪ Present findings on your topic
   ▪ Highlight an intervention or program similar to yours
   ▪ Address issues about your population

✓ *A word of warning:* Too often students have spent many hours, even days, in the library and come to us in frustration because they have nothing to show for their efforts. Do not make the same mistake. Start your search early and regularly seek help. Consult with your librarians and instructors frequently. Remember: *Seek assistance at the first sign that you are not getting anywhere.*

REMINDER:

> Be sure that you know how to conduct a literature search using electronic databases on-line or in the library. Do not simply do a search on the Internet. Ask reference librarians for assistance. They can save you much time.

A.   CONDUCT A LITERATURE SEARCH

The following directions will guide you step-by-step through the process of locating literature relevant to your research question. Remember to record what you have done and where you have looked.

1) Ask your course instructor if he or she can recommend any faculty members who are knowledgeable about the topic of your study or population of interest. Talk to suggested faculty members, your field instructor, and other people at your agency to obtain their recommendations for references. Sometimes, locating the right person can give you the bulk of your references.

   Indicate with whom you talked, when, and the results.

2) Begin searching the literature by choosing key search words.

List several options for key search words. (Ask your professor and/or librarian for their advice.)

3) List the databases you will use for your search. Obtain information on how to access them, if you do not know already.

4) Go to your first database and begin entering the requested information.

    a) Set the computer search so that it returns the abstract for each reference. This will help you to do the initial gleaning of the list.

    b) Limit your search to the last five years to start. If that does not generate enough references, do not be too quick to go back more years. Rather, reconsider your search words.

    c) If you use the PsychLit abstracts, in the P.T. field (publication type) you can specify empirical study and it will limit the search to return empirical studies only.

5) Search!

If the search results include significantly more than about 40 or 50 references, you will need to further narrow your search words or dates so that you have a manageable list of references to review. Do not hesitate to get assistance with this task.

Reference database software such as EndNote® or RefWorks® may be available through your university. These programs can search databases on the internet and assist you as you write your paper and organize your references. They can also save your search strategies, allow you to link your references to full-text articles on the web, and format your in-text citations and reference page in the reference style required by your instructor.

6) Once you have a successful search list, read through it several times.

    a) Read the abstracts in the list and highlight references that appear to be on target with your question.

    b) Highlight any article that is titled "A Review [or Synthesis or Meta-Analysis] of the Literature." It will provide an overview of the literature related to your topic and can save you much time.

7) Submit the results of your computer search to your instructor for feedback, circling the references you intend to use and starring the empirical articles. Be sure to write your research question on the top of your computer search list.

8) Select and locate the 10 sources you and your instructor have decided will be most relevant. You should start to track down your literature very soon. Many sources will be available online or in your library. Some sources, however, will have to be obtained from another library through Interlibrary Loan, which may require as much as two or three weeks.

9) Finally, when you have some literature in hand, among those sources that are most closely related to your research question, choose the most current and examine the authors' references at the end. This will help you identify other relevant sources.

B.   EVALUATE AND CRITIQUE THE LITERATURE

Your written literature review summarizes and evaluates each author's work as it relates to your study. A literature review is not a series of long, direct quotations, nor is it a list of summaries of each source, although that may be how you initially organize your information. Your literature review should integrate and synthesize the information from the sources you have selected. Organize your literature review by topic, not by author or source of information. Many students find it helpful to develop an outline of their literature review topics, including what various authors have said or found about each or the topics. Writing a literature review is time-intensive and will require multiple drafts with revisions.

For each source, the following sets of questions will help as you explore the literature. The first set is for use with empirical articles, the second set with nonempirical articles. We recommend that you answer these questions for each source you plan to cite in your study. We have also included examples for both types of articles.

A NOTE ABOUT CRITIQUING EMPIRICAL STUDIES

As noted earlier, if you find an article or book that is a current review of the literature, review of recent empirical work, compendium of best practices, or meta-analysis of research studies relevant to your topic, yes, you are fortunate indeed. However, bear in mind that such finds may be narrowly focused or biased (and exclude research on other interventions worth considering). Alas, critical thinking skills are still required. These articles may include studies with limited or no information about the rigor of the research designs (published ≠ quality; even peer-reviewed does not guarantee quality).

There are a variety of rating systems that people have used to evaluate the quality of research studies. Authors of articles using meta-analysis will generally describe their method of evaluation. Others can be found online, such as the CDC's efficacy criteria for selecting a behavioral intervention as a best practice (http://www.cdc.gov/hiv/topics/research/prs/ efficacy_best-evidence.htm).

All of the rating systems share two primary emphases that should also be yours as you review your empirical articles: measurement and design. Essentially you want to evaluate each study on the extent to which the authors used valid and reliable measurement and the extent to which they utilized a research design that allowed them to infer that the findings were a result of the intervention and not other factors.

Use the following guide as you review each study.

FOR EMPIRICAL STUDIES:

Author and Date:
Title:
Citation Information:

a) What is the purpose of this study and how is it related to your study?

b) What theory or theories or models (if any) does the author use in this study? How might you apply these to the topic of your study?

c) In a brief paragraph describe *how* the sample was obtained. Who was (and was not) targeted for inclusion in the study? What response rate did the study have? What was the attrition (drop out) rate over the course of the intervention? And what biases if any did that present? Was there a follow-up post intervention—how long after, with what participation level?

d) Include a brief description of the sample (size, gender, race, age, socioeconomic class, special characteristics), paying close attention to the inclusion and representation of people of color, a group frequently underrepresented in research. (For example, are people of color included in sufficient numbers, or are several groups simply pooled together with only white and nonwhite comparisons reported? Groups reported as nonwhite do not tell us anything about specific minority groups.)

e) What are the major concepts in the study and the variables chosen to represent each concept?

f) Indicate the specific measures used (operationalization) for each of the major variables in the article that are relevant to your study. Begin with the dependent variables if dependent and independent variables are included. How did the authors address the validity and reliability of their measures? Do they discuss the extent to which the measures have been used and/or tested previously with this population?

g) If the article is an evaluation of an intervention, briefly describe the intervention. How were people trained to implement the intervention? What was the process, if any, to ensure that staff carried out the intervention as designed (i.e., treatment integrity)?

h) Which of the following research designs was used and what were its limitations? What limitations did the authors report? Can you identify others?

- Single-case (one individual or group, often with pre and posttest measures)
- Fixed groups (experimental treatment group and a selected group for comparison)
- Randomly assigned groups (experimental treatment and control or alternative treatment groups)

i) Describe the method of data collection.

j) Summarize the findings of the study in two or three sentences.

k) What will you apply from this study to your own? How might you use its strengths or compensate for its limitations?

SAMPLE CRITIQUE FOR EMPIRICAL STUDIES

Author and Date: Mokuau, N., Braun, K. L., Wong, L. K., Higuchi, P., & Gotay, C. C. (2008).
Title: Development of a family intervention for Native Hawaiian women with cancer: A pilot study.
Citation Information: *Social Work (53)*1, 9-19.

a) **What is the purpose of this study and how is it related to your study?**

Purpose of study: to assess feasibility and effectiveness of a culturally appropriate intervention for cancer patients and their families. The intervention provides information to increase patients' ability to cope with cancer, resulting in a higher quality of life.

How it relates to my study: I want to evaluate an intervention for Mexican-American cancer caregivers. This study is similar to what I hope to do, with a different underserved population. I can look at how the authors conceptualized their intervention, designed the study and consider the instruments that the researchers used.

b) **What theory or theories or models (if any) does the author use in this study? How might you apply these to the topic of your study?**

The authors developed a culturally appropriate intervention and then evaluated its effectiveness. The intervention is based on the premise that among Native Hawaiians, cancer is experienced in the family and intervention should focus on the family and the cultural values of the group.

c) **In a brief paragraph describe *how* the sample was obtained. Who was (and was not) targeted for inclusion in the study? What response rate did the study have? What was the attrition (drop out) rate over the course of the intervention? And what biases if any did that present? Was there a follow-up post intervention—how long after, with what participation level?**

The target population is Native Hawaiian women with cancer because these women experience late detection of their cancer at advanced stages. They are also known to have behavioral risk factors and genetic predisposition.

The authors used a variety of recruitment strategies (see p. 12 in article). Twelve women volunteered for the study; two women withdrew before the intervention. The authors assessed that the withdrawals did not affect the results. There was no follow up reported.

d) **Include a brief description of the sample (size, gender, race, age, socioeconomic class, special characteristics), paying close attention to the inclusion and representation of people of color, a group frequently underrepresented in research. (For example, are people of color included in sufficient numbers, or are several groups simply pooled** together with only white and nonwhite comparisons reported? Groups reported as nonwhite do not tell us anything about specific minority groups.)

All of the participants were women; the average age was about 55 years; they had various types of cancer, with breast cancer being the most common.

One to three family members were invited to participate in the intervention, with an average of two family members per cancer patient. Family members were spouses and adult children; half of the family members in the study were male.

e) **What are the major concepts in the study and the variables chosen to represent each concept?**

CONCEPTS:	DEPENDENT VARIABLES:
Lack of information about cancer, treatment	Cancer knowledge
Lack of skills in talking with doctors	Self-efficacy
Family help, support for the cancer patient	Self-efficacy
Stress and quality of life	Psychological distress
	INDEPENDENT VARIABLE:
Culturally appropriate, family-oriented, group versus individual focus	Intervention developed for study

f) **Indicate the specific measures used (operationalization) for each of the major variables in the article that are relevant to your study. Begin with the dependent variables if dependent and independent variables are included. How did the authors address the validity and reliability of their measures? Do they discuss the extent to which the measures have been used and/or tested previously with this population?**

DEPENDENT VARIABLES:
   Cancer knowledge: authors constructed an instrument from the Cancer Survival Toolkit; 15 items scored correct or incorrect.
   Self-efficacy: participants were asked about their confidence in accessing information and services for cancer, talking to medical professionals, etc.; 12 items; constructed by authors.
   Family coping behaviors: measured by the Family Crisis-Oriented Personal Evaluation Scale (F-COPES); 30 item, Likert-style instrument.
   Psychological distress: measured by the Brief Symptom Inventory (BSI); 53 items with index for global severity.

Reliability and validity of all instruments are addressed by authors in the article (see p. 13).

For independent variable see intervention below.

g) **If the article is an evaluation of an intervention, briefly describe the intervention. How were people trained to implement the intervention? What was the process, if any, to ensure adherence to the intervention (i.e., ensure all staff carried it out as intended)?**

INTERVENTION: Delivered by MSW social workers, six home sessions over three months. MSWs provided educational materials (brochures, etc.), how to access information through the internet (Cancer Information Service, etc.), communication skills, discussion of family roles and responsibilities. One of the MSWs was a cancer specialist.

h) **What was the research design and what were its limitations? What limitations did the authors report? Can you identify others?**

The authors used a one group pretest-posttest design.

Participants in the sample of 12 were randomly assigned to intervention and control groups. (Note that the control group also received some intervention sessions due to the ethical issue of withholding the intervention from some of the participants.)

i) **Describe the method of data collection.**

Data were collected using the measures above, plus a demographic form, at the first session of the intervention (pretest measures) and at the final session at the end of the three-month intervention (posttest measures). Authors do not say specifically how the instruments were administered, face-to-face interviews or pencil and paper by the participants.

j) **Summarize the findings of the study in two or three sentences.**

Authors found that the intervention group did better overall than the control group on the outcome measures (dependent variables). They used t-tests to examine the differences between the two groups for statistical significance.

Authors also report the results of the feasibility of the study (see pp. 15-16.) I will not be assessing feasibility.

k) **What will you apply from this study to your own? How might you use its strengths or compensate for its limitations?**

Intervention is similar to mine, targeting an underserved population.

Authors support the rationale for a culturally appropriate intervention. They clearly describe the intervention.

Authors used multiple recruitment and retention strategies. I can use these ideas in my study since I am concerned about attrition.

Small sample size limits the confidence in findings. This will be true for my study. The authors assigned volunteers to treatment and control groups. I won't have a control group. This is a limitation of my study and I will have to consider threats to internal validity.

I will use a pretest and posttest with the participants in my study. I will be able to use t-tests for my data analysis, comparing pre- to post-test scores.

Measures used may be appropriate for my study – write to authors to see if they will share the instruments they developed (demographic, cancer knowledge, and self-efficacy).

FOR NONEMPIRICAL ARTICLES:

These articles will most likely be expository articles: discussions of theory, summaries of many other studies, or general overviews of the topic you are studying. For each article you plan to use, provide the citation and ask yourself the following questions:

Author and Date:
Title:
Citation Information:

a) What is the main topic of this article?

b) What information does it provide that is helpful for a better understanding of the topic or helpful in the actual design of your study?

SAMPLE CRITIQUE FOR NONEMPIRICAL STUDIES

Author and Date: Harrigan, M. P. & Koerin, B. B. (2007).
Title: Long-distance care giving: Personal realities and practice implications.
Citation Information: *Reflections: Narratives of Professional Helping, (13)*2, 5-16.

a) **What is the main topic of this article?**

The article presents issues and challenges faced by long-distance caregivers, family members who are not living in the same location as the person requiring care. Suggestions are made for social workers working with care recipients and long-distance caregivers.

b) **What information does it provide that is helpful for a better understanding of the topic or helpful in the actual design of your study?**

My study will assess caregiver burden as well as resources and supports available to caregivers. This article presents and discusses some of the challenges to family members who do not live near the care recipient, as well as the benefits from long-distance family members becoming involved with local caregivers and resources for the care recipients. The article helps me understand some of the feelings that caregivers experience – guilt, grief, uncertainty, fear – as part of the care giving role. It also suggests that long-distance caregivers may have more of a role in caring than we might think. Since many of my participants may have family and friends living in Mexico, it might be interesting to assess what role long-distance caregivers have and if they serve as support systems to the local caregivers.

REMINDER:

When writing the research proposal, the text is written in future tense, indicating what you will be doing. When writing the final research report, you will have completed the study. The report will describe and explain what you have done, so the report will be written in past tense. If you complete your study, when you write the report, be sure to change the tense to indicate that you have completed the study.

C. WRITE THE INTRODUCTION SECTION

Before you start writing, check with your course instructor for the reference style that she or he expects you to follow. Much social work literature uses the American Psychological Association (APA) reference style.

This is where the reference database software that we noted in Section A, Part 5 would be quite valuable. The programs format your in-text citations and reference page in the reference style required by your instructor.

You will save much time and energy if you use the expected format and style as you conduct the project and write early drafts. We know from experience that it takes less effort now to put the paper into the correct style than to revise it later. The library, your university's writing center, and online resources can provide style manuals to guide you.

Once you have received feedback from your course instructor, you are ready to write the first draft of the introduction and literature review sections of your paper. As you complete the other steps of your study, you may find more information that you want to include.

Both the Introduction section and Literature Review section rely on the sources that you have identified. In the Introduction, you use literature to establish the importance of the topic and the value of your study which will address a gap in the existing literature on the topic. The Introduction also contains a statement clarifying the purpose of the study.

The Introduction section of your paper should be about one page. Outline the scope and significance, relevance, and purpose of your study, identifying the articles that support your points.

1) Scope and significance of the problem or issue

2) Relevance to social work

3) Specification of the research question (purpose of the study)

D.   WRITE THE LITERATURE REVIEW SECTION

The Literature Review section of your paper provides a context for your study and presents a synthesis and evaluation of prior empirical work on your topic. It justifies the research question you have chosen and the study you will conduct.

Your literature review should use existing literature to:

- Introduce your topic and provide a background for your study
- Describe the context, causes, and responses to the topic you are studying
- Introduce theoretical frameworks
- Define variables and key terms
- Present and critique measures and methods used in prior studies
- Critically review findings of prior empirical work

The final paragraph of your literature review should:

- Summarize and critically evaluate what is currently known about the topic
- Identify contradictory information and gaps in the existing literature
- Restate the purpose of your proposed study.

1) Make a plan for how you will present related literature. What are the main topics you will cover in your review?

   Organize the topics in a meaningful way so that your discussion of the literature has a logical flow. Try beginning with broad, general information and move to more specific information. Use an expository article to make a particular point and then an empirical article to provide evidence for that point.

   Outline the main topics of your literature review on separate pages. Once you have the main topic areas, you can expand the outline by filling in information from your sources. When possible, use multiple sources to support your points. Above all, avoid presenting a summary of each source one after the other.

2) Using your expanded outline as a guide, write your review of the literature (minimum of four pages). Use subheadings that match your topics to help the reader follow your outline. At the end of the literature review state your research question again in its final form.

Writing a literature review is difficult for even experienced researchers, so don't become discouraged. Most people find synthesizing what they have read to be the most difficult part of the research process. We believe that the best way to learn how to write a good literature review is to read other literature reviews. Reading many literature reviews will help you develop the skills that you need to write a good review. So when you feel stuck, read literature reviews to see how others have organized and presented theirs.

Keep in mind that as you continue through the workbook and the design of your study, you will probably locate other sources that you will include in the final draft of your paper.

Remember that you have an ethical responsibility to cite all your sources properly, to indicate when you are using an author's exact words, and to make it clear when you are paraphrasing an author's ideas. If you are uncertain about proper documentation, ask your instructor for assistance or go to your university's writing center.

Submit drafts of the Introduction and Literature Review sections to your course instructor along with your proposed study design (see Chapter 5: Choosing Your Methodology).

We have provided an example of an annotated literature review on the following pages to help you write your literature review.

E.   ANNOTATED EXAMPLE OF A LITERATURE REVIEW

INTRODUCTION

.

.

.

indicates additional text removed for the sake of brevity

[1] Establishes importance of the issue

[1] Antiretrovirals (ARVs), particularly protease inhibitors, are potent agents in reducing the viral load in HIV-positive individuals. However, these positive effects can be short-lived in many patients if they do not take the antiretroviral medications as prescribed. Poor patient adherence to these drugs can rapidly lead to resistance and negate the benefits of combination therapy. In addition, as a result of poor adherence, public health is threatened as the virus becomes resistant to antiretroviral therapy.

[2] States value of the study

[2] Recent research on adherence to antiretrovirals suggests that adherence rates greater than 90 percent are necessary to maintain suppression of HIV (Patterson et al., 1999). Unfortunately, numerous studies have documented low rates of adherence to antiretroviral medication among HIV-positive individuals (Leslie, 2000).

[3] Indicates what is missing from the literature

[3] While researchers have sought to determine factors related to adherence among this group, very few efforts have been directed at designing and evaluating approaches to assisting individuals in improving adherence. [2] This area of research is absolutely critical to the development of an effective response to the HIV epidemic (Michael, 2000).

[4] States purpose of the study

[4] This study seeks to evaluate the effectiveness of a bi-weekly phone counseling approach in increasing adherence to antiretroviral medications among HIV+ persons.

[5] Introduces theoretical connection

[5] The intervention model takes into account individual stages of change readiness and begins the intervention at the patient's level.

BACKGROUND

HIV in the United States

[6] Provides context
with historical data

[6] Due to improved antiretroviral therapies and treatment, death rates and opportunistic infections associated with AIDS have declined since late 1995, however, the estimated total number of persons living with AIDS has steadily increased. According to the most recent HIV/AIDS Surveillance Report, a total of 665,357 persons with AIDS have been reported to the Centers for Disease Control (CDC) through 30 June 1998. Of these, 401,028 (60%) deaths have been reported. This report indicates that the estimated number of persons living with AIDS is currently greater than 264,000 (Centers for Disease Control and Prevention, 1998).

Advances in Antiretroviral Therapy

Several significant advances in the approach to antiretroviral therapy have led to the recently observed changes in the AIDS death rates and incidence of opportunistic infections.

.

.

.

Adherence

[7] Conceptualization:
definition of key terms

[7] *Defining adherence.* Adherence has become a popular term since it may be viewed as less judgmental than the term compliance. However, the terms "compliance" and "adherence" are used interchangeably in the literature (Mehta et al., 1997). As reviewed by Morris and Schulz (1992), patient medication compliance may be defined as a process or an outcome. The outcome-oriented definition is commonly employed by adherence researchers. This approach focuses on a defined outcome as a result of a patient performing a specific action, such as taking medication. It is quantified by the percentage of time that a patient takes her or his medication as prescribed. Currently there is no accepted minimum percentage level or outcome-oriented definition of medication adherence for patients with HIV.

[8] Prior empirical work

[8] *Adherence in chronic illnesses.* Rates of adherence with long term medications for chronic conditions have consistently been found to average around 50%, regardless of illness or setting (Donovan & Blake, 1992). Medication adherence is well studied for chronic disease states such as diabetes, hypertension, tuberculosis, mental illness, and others (Morris & Schulz, 1992).

Adherence among HIV+ Patients. Data regarding medication adherence in HIV-infected patients first appeared in the literature in

47

the early 1990s (Samuels et al., 1990). The early studies centered around adherence to single agent antiretroviral regimens involving zidovudine (Samuels et al., 1990; Morse et al., 1991; Samet et al., 1992; Broers et al., 1994; Wall et al., 1995; Geletko et al., 1996). However, over the past two years there has been renewed interest in evaluating adherence issues in this population due to the increased utilization of combination therapy that requires patients to take complex, multidrug medication regimens with varied dosing schedules.

.

.

.

Recent medication adherence studies in HIV patients. Recent medication studies indicate that 21 to 43% of all patients regularly miss doses of their antiretroviral or opportunistic infection prophylaxis medications.

.

.

.

[9] Operationalization: Measures used in prior empirical work

Measuring Adherence

[9] Adherence typically has been measured both directly and indirectly (Morris & Schulz, 1992). Direct measurements involve detection of certain chemicals in body fluid levels, whereas indirect measures include prescription refills, pill counts, medication self-reports, and even the subjective impressions of health care providers (cf. Morse et al., 1991). Direct measurements, while objective and less biased, may be influenced by individual patient pharmacokinetics and time of medication dosing. Additionally, these methods do not accurately reflect what activity has taken place over time, are generally impractical in many settings, and often lack established reference ranges relative to specific dosing activity.

[10] Critique of measures

[10] Indirect measures such as patient interviews and self-reports are among the more common methods; however, they usually overestimate compliance despite the skill of the interviewer or design of the self-report form (Cramer et al., 1989).

.

.

.

[11] Summarizes what is currently known regarding interventions to improve adherence

Efforts to Improve Adherence

[11] While it is known that adherence is lower when the regimen is complex and of long duration, requires changes in lifestyle, and is inconvenient and expensive (all factors inherent in antiretroviral medication regimens), there is sparse information regarding the best means of enhancing adherence (Eldred et al.,

1997; Urquhart, 1992; Scaler et al., 1994). Most interventions can be categorized as educational, behavioral, or a combination of the two. Educational strategies, involving written and/or verbal communication, are based on an information model of adherence and suggest that patients given sufficient information (regarding the disease, medications, and side effects) will demonstrate increased adherence.

.

.

.

Behavioral interventions, such as medication calendars, refill reminders (by phone or mail), and special medication containers have also increased adherence rates (Morris & Schulz, 1992). Most promising, however, has been the combination of educational and behavioral interventions.

[12] Critically analyzes findings

[12] The 1996 review of randomized trials of interventions to improve adherence completed by Haynes, McKibbon, and Kanani stands as the most comprehensive review of that literature to date.

.

.

.

Only one study was located that utilized an experimental design to evaluate the effectiveness of an intervention to increase adherence to an antiretroviral, ZDV. Sorenson et al. (1998) evaluated eight weeks of onsite dispensing to 25 patients enrolled in a methadone clinic and compared outcomes to those randomly assigned to a usual care group. The researchers found no statistically significant differences in self-report of adherence during the intervention or at the one month follow-up.

In adherence research it is easy to lose track of the ultimate goal beyond improved adherence, that of clinical benefit. Six of the interventions reviewed by Haynes et al. (1996) resulted in clinical improvement, with only four demonstrating improvement in both adherence and clinical outcome, further emphasizing the researchers' point that the increases in adherence were generally not substantial. Likewise, the Sorenson et al. (1998) study found no significant clinical benefit of onsite dispensing (using mean corpuscular volume as an indicator). Haynes et al. (1996) cited the urgent need for testing of further innovations in treatment methods, innovations that "are more likely to occur if investigators join across clinical disciplines to tackle low adherence" (p. 386).

SUMMARY

[13] Reviews key points of literature review

[13] Near total adherence for individuals taking antiretrovirals is absolutely essential. Unfortunately, only 57-79% of persons taking antiretrovirals achieve adherence levels of 80% or more, a level that most clinicians and researchers realize is unacceptable for this population in its fight against HIV. Equally unfortunate is that, constrained by a relatively short time of investigation, the factors related to adherence have not been well-identified. Neither have the few tests of health behavior models been well supported. Even more unfortunate is that evaluations of efforts to improve adherence among HIV+ individuals have been rare.

[14] Restates purpose of proposed study

[14] Utilizing a randomized wait-list control group experimental design in two sites, chosen specifically to test the intervention in settings already providing HIV care (a university-based HIV clinic and a community-based pharmacy specializing in HIV care), we intend to:

1) provide and evaluate services designed to increase levels of adherence among 50 individuals; and
2) assess risk factors for nonadherence by examining the link between adherence and sociodemographic variables, disease state and perceived risk and threat of illness, intention to adhere, medication regimen, social supports, substance abuse, and emotional health.

Written by Alex Westerfelt, Ph.D. and Melinda Lacy, Pharm.D.

ONLINE DATABASES

Abstracts in Social Gerontology includes bibliographic records covering essential areas related to social gerontology, including the psychology of aging, elder abuse, society and the elderly, and other areas.

Academic Search Complete is a comprehensive scholarly, multi-disciplinary full text database, with more than 5,300 full text periodicals, including 4,400 peer-reviewed journals.

AgeLine contains detailed summaries of publications about older adults and aging from the gerontology collection of AARP's Research Information Center, as well as selected articles from 300 magazines and journals.

Alcohol and Alcohol Problems Science Database covers all aspects of alcohol abuse and alcoholism.

American Psychological Association's website on empirically supported treatments provides brief descriptions of various psychotherapies that have met basic scientific standards for effectiveness.

Child Abuse, Child Welfare, and Adoption provides a bibliographic resource on the maltreatment of children. Includes reports on completed on continuing research, as well as descriptions of service programs and prevention and treatment strategies.

Child Care & Early Education Research Connection from the National Center for Children in Poverty at Columbia University is a multidisciplinary collection of resources for researchers, practitioners and policy makers in child care and early education.

Child Welfare Information Gateway from the Children's Bureau, Administration for Children and Families, U.S. Department of Health and Human Services, provides access to information and resources to help protect children and strengthen families. Topics include family services; reporting, preventing, and responding to child abuse; child care services; adoption; statistics, laws, and policies; cultural sensitivity; funding and organizational issues; and more.

Cochrane Library is an electronic publication designed to supply high quality evidence to inform people providing and receiving health care, and those responsible for research, teaching, funding and administration of health care at all levels. Cochrane reviews represent the highest level of evidence on which to base clinical treatment decisions.

Criminal Justice Abstracts provides indexing of major international journals, books, dissertations and reports in criminology and related disciplines. Subjects covered include: crime trends, crime prevention and deterrence, juvenile delinquency, juvenile justice, police, courts, punishment and sentencing.

ERIC *(Education Resources Information Center)* provides a digital library of education-related resources. Covers research documents, journal articles, technical reports, program descriptions and evaluations, and curricular materials in the field of education.

HAPI *(Health and Psychosocial Instruments)* provides bibliographic access and descriptions of tests, manuals, rating scales and other instruments used to assess health and behavior. Assists researchers in locating instruments used in the health fields, psychosocial sciences, organizational behavior, and library and information science.

National Guideline Clearinghouse website is a public resource for evidence-based clinical practice guidelines. www.guidelines.gov

National Institute of Drug Abuse website disseminates research related to drug abuse and addiction in order to significantly improve prevention, treatment and policy.

Mental Measurements Yearbook contains full text information about and reviews of English-language standardized tests covering educational skills, personality, vocational aptitude, psychology, and related areas.

NCJRS *(National Criminal Justice Reference Service)* provides an information clearinghouse for people involved with research, policy, and practice related to criminal and juvenile justice, and drug control.

PAIS International includes abstracts covering the full range of political, social, and public policy issues.

PsycINFO covers the professional and academic literature in psychology and related disciplines including (but not limited to): anthropology, business, education, law, linguistics, medicine, nursing, pharmacology, physiology, psychiatry, and sociology.

Social Sciences Citation Index is a multidisciplinary index to the journal literature of the social sciences.

Social Services Abstracts provides bibliographic coverage of current research focused on social work, human services, and related areas, including social welfare, social policy, and community development.

Social Work Abstracts is produced by the National Association of Social Workers. Sample topics include homelessness, AIDS, child and family welfare, aging, substance abuse, legislation, and community organization.

Sociological Abstracts indexes and abstracts the international literature in sociology and related disciplines in the social and behavioral sciences.

Acknowledgement: We would like to thank John J. Dillard, MA, MS, Social Work and Social Sciences Librarian at the University of Texas-Arlington, for his help in compiling this list.

CHAPTER 5

CHOOSING YOUR METHODOLOGY & DEVELOPING A TIMELINE

Having examined the literature, you know some of the methods of study others have used to explore your topic. Now you must decide the particular method you will use to conduct your own investigation. This workbook offers four options: survey research, qualitative research, single-case design research, and outcome evaluation.

In most instances, to the extent that you have narrowed and adequately specified your research question, you will have obligated yourself to a particular method of study. If you are uncertain, review your research question. Inherent in most research questions is an indication of the purpose of the research to be undertaken. Remember: Purpose directs method. Ask yourself what the purpose of your study is.

A word about the use of existing data. Many times, agencies have existing data that were previously collected and may be available to you for your study. They might have been collected as part of a survey or program evaluation and not yet analyzed. Using existing data can save time and be less costly than collecting your own. Of course, there are disadvantages to using existing data. Existing data may not have the precise information that you are seeking, may not use the best measures, or may have inaccuracies or missing data that will limit your study. If you are considering using existing data, talk with your instructor to think through if it will meet your needs.

A. DETERMINE THE PURPOSE OF YOUR STUDY

Check to see which of the following best applies to your question.

- ❑ If the purpose of your study is to document the magnitude of a problem or the quantity of various characteristics (for example, how satisfied people are with services or how many people need a particular service) or determine individual ratings based on scaled measures (for example, parenting skills), then you will use the survey method. You may also explore existing data that relied on the survey method for data collection. In either case, go to Chapter 6.

❑ If the purpose of your study is to gain a deeper understanding of how participants have experienced a particular event or state (for example, homelessness), then qualitative interviewing usually will be your method of choice. This is also true when exploring something about which little is known (for example, how terminally ill cancer patients perceive home visits by social work case managers). Go to Chapter 7.

❑ If the purpose of your study is to evaluate how an intervention affects a single client system (individual, family, program, or community), then single-case design will most likely be your method of choice. Go to Chapter 8.

❑ If the purpose of your study is to evaluate how an intervention or program affects multiple clients, then an outcome evaluation is your method of choice. Again, your agency may already have existing data that can be used for an outcome evaluation. Go to Chapter 9.

This is not to say there is only one right method for each research question. The choice of method depends greatly on the exact specification of what you want to know. Because each research question is unique, we cannot give more specific guidance regarding which method to choose, and we encourage you to talk with your course instructor for further help. Prepare for a discussion with your course instructor by thinking about the purpose of your study and what you have learned from reviewing the literature.

We think it is important to note that many research questions benefit from a mixed-methods approach, although we will grant that you will not see this done very often. And while we don't recommend a mixed-methods approach for a person's first research study, we mention it here to emphasize the importance of being clear about your research purpose before choosing a method, and also to emphasize the value of the mixed-methods approach to increasing practice knowledge.

For example, in asking what factors seem to be related to turnover among social workers in nursing homes, a survey would be an appropriate research method. However, in a review of the literature one might find that earlier studies of nursing home staff (not just social workers) identified "feeling empowered" as a factor reported by staff in nursing homes with lower turnover. As another part of your study then, you could include a focus group of social workers to explore the concept of empowerment and how that relates to their job satisfaction. Or you could do the focus group first followed by a survey, based on information collected in the focus group. In our opinion a mixed-methods approach is often ideal but too seldom used.

Write a sentence or two combining the purpose of your study and the method you have chosen below.

Purpose of Your Study and Method:

Please refer to the appropriate method chapter of the workbook.

B.   DEVELOP YOUR PROPOSED TIMELINE

The next step is to plan the dates by which you need to complete each step of the research project. We recommend that you work backwards from the final completion date. We provide a timeline on page 56 for conducting a research study as part of a one- or two-semester course. You may have more or less time to conduct your study, so plan accordingly.

Enter the dates for completing each stage of your proposed study on the timeline provided on the next page.

C.   SUBMIT PROPOSED STUDY TO YOUR COURSE INSTRUCTOR

Submit drafts of the Introduction and Literature Review sections of your paper along with the purpose, proposed method, and timeline for your study to your course instructor for his or her feedback.

TIMELINE

Stages of Conducting Your Research Project	One Semester Timeline	Two Semester Timeline	Completion Dates
1. **Develop Your Research Question and Human Subjects Review Application** *See Workbook Chapters 1, 2, 3 & 11*	1 to 2 weeks	4 weeks	_____
2. **Conduct Literature Review, Select Research Design and Sample Design** *See Workbook Chapters 4, 5 & 10*	2 to 3 weeks	6 weeks	_____
3. **Develop Measurement Instruments** *See Workbook Chapter 6, 7, 8 or 9, depending on your method*	2 weeks	4 weeks	_____
4. **Pilot Measurement Instruments*** *See Workbook Chapter 6, 7, 8 or 9, depending on your method*	1 week	2 week	_____
5. **Collect Your Data** *See Workbook Chapter 6, 7, 8 or 9, depending on your method*	4 weeks	6 weeks	_____
6. **Analyze Your Data** *See Workbook Chapter 12, 13 or 14, depending on your method*	2 weeks	4 weeks	_____
7. **Prepare Final Research Report** *See Workbook Chapter 15*	2 weeks	4 weeks	_____
Submit Final Research Report		**Report Due:**	_____

* Remember, you must have IRB approval even before piloting your instrument.

CHAPTER 6

SURVEY RESEARCH

RECOMMENDED ARTICLE:
DiFranks, N. N. (2008). Social workers and the NASW Code of Ethics: Belief, behavior, disjuncture. *Social Work, (53)*2, 167-176.

Researchers rely more on survey methods than any other method. With appropriate sampling procedures, researchers utilize surveys to gather a wealth of information about individuals, families, groups, and communities. Options for the design of survey studies are addressed below. This chapter of the workbook is intended to guide you through each of the steps necessary to design a survey study.

Now that you have completed a review of the literature and chosen your method of inquiry, you are ready to develop a research instrument and plan its method of administration.

A. TRANSLATE CONCEPTS AND VARIABLES INTO MEASURES

REMINDER:
Review your methods text regarding operationalization and measurement.

In your literature review you identified major concepts and variables from other studies and indicated the measures (indicators) chosen for each of them. Now you will develop the indicators for each variable you intend to measure.

In the case of scales that are used in studies and cited in articles, you may have to locate the article that contains the actual items of the scale and includes information about the development and testing of that scale. The article will be listed in the references of the study article you have read. Sometimes you may need to call or write the author to see the actual scale. Some scales are copyrighted and can be used only if a fee is paid for their use.

If you plan to use an existing scale, allow time to ascertain these things and obtain a copy of the scale.

There are also texts which include many scales such as Fischer and Corcoran's (2006) *Measures for Clinical Practice* and Jordan and Franklin's (2003) *Clinical Assessment for Social Workers*. These usually can be found in your library's reference section. For additional suggestions see Rubin and Babbie's (2008) *Research Methods for Social Work*.

Finally, in addition to the other resources available, don't overlook your agency's resources. They may have instruments that are available for your use.

If, on the other hand, you develop your own instrumentation, allow time to share it with others and receive feedback.

First, let's consider what measures have been used.

1) What are the key variables of interest in your study? Drawing from your literature review, how have others measured each of these?

   On the following page, specify each variable, then complete the information in the table. If the agency has measured these variables before, include their measures or questions.

2) Your intended measures:

   a) Circle the measures that you plan to use. Relative to scales, indicate how much time it will take to complete the scale, either by interview or self-administered. If you do not plan to use any of the reviewed measures, continue to Part b; otherwise go to Part d.

   b) If none of the above measures seems appropriate, or if you want to develop measures of your own in addition to conventional measures you have selected, indicate why and the measures you propose.

VARIABLE AUTHOR & DATE	MEASURE	BRIEF DESCRIPTION	SCALE RELIABILITY & VALIDITY	HOW COLLECTED & TIME INVOLVED
1)				
2)				
3)				

c) Don't assume that because a scale is cited often or copyrighted, it is bias-free. Evaluate whether your chosen measures have a cultural bias in terms of age; race; gender; social class; physical, mental or emotional ability; or sexual orientation. In the case of validated scales, with whom and with what age group have the scales been tested for validity and reliability?

d) Discuss potential limitations of your measures relative to reliability and validity.

B.   CONSTRUCT YOUR RESEARCH QUESTIONNAIRE

REMINDER:
Review your text regarding construction of questionnaires.

You are now ready to construct the questionnaire for your study. The measures you have detailed above will make up part of the questionnaire, but you will probably want to include other items as well. The following questions are intended to help you further develop the questionnaire. If you are planning an online survey, you should still create a written draft of your questionnaire using the steps below.

1) Check with agency staff and see what other questions they would like to include. Indicate to whom you talked and their ideas.

2) Check with clients and see what other questions they would suggest including. Indicate to whom you talked and their ideas.

3) Indicate demographic information you wish to collect, such as age, race, gender, marital/partner status, education, employment, or income.

4) Draft a copy of your questionnaire, including each question word-for-word, in the order you intend to present the items.

5) Refine each item on the questionnaire to accomplish the following:

- ❑ For close-ended questions, exhaustive and mutually exclusive responses.
- ❑ No double-barreled questions.
- ❑ No biased items or terms.
- ❑ No leading questions.
- ❑ Clear instructions if questionnaire is to be self-administered.

6) Revise your draft so that you can answer "yes" to the following questions:

- ❑ Is the questionnaire uncluttered?
- ❑ Is it as brief as possible?
- ❑ Is the order of questions appropriate (first questions capture the participant's interest; sensitive questions come later)?
- ❑ Are appropriate contingency (also called skip) questions used so that people are not asked irrelevant questions?
- ❑ Have you formatted the questionnaire in a way that will be easy for you to analyze and tabulate?
- ❑ Is the language appropriate for the participants?
- ❑ What reading level is your questionnaire written at? What reading level do most of your respondents read at?

7) Use your word processing software for an analysis of reading level.

(For example, in MS Word® go to Tools/ Spelling and Grammar/ Options/ check both boxes, "Check grammar with spelling" and "Show readability statistics." When the spell check is complete, a pop-up window will show the reading level and readability (on a scale of easy to hard, 1 to 100) of your document. The readability statistics are based on the average *number of **words** per sentence* and the average *number of **syllables** per word*. This chapter, for example, scores at 47% and an eleventh grade reading level.)

To lower the reading level of your document, use words with fewer syllables and make your sentences shorter. Aim for a seventh grade reading level in most instances.

8) Give the questionnaire to at least two people to critique (your field instructor, other agency staff, or peers—but not clients yet).

9) Complete a revised version of your questionnaire, incorporating the feedback you received from others, and submit it to your course instructor to approve before you pilot it.

C. PLAN HOW TO ADMINISTER YOUR QUESTIONNAIRE

REMINDER:
Review your text regarding options for administering questionnaires.

Survey research can be conducted in several ways. You must decide if the questionnaire will be self-administered by the participant or administered by an interviewer who will record the participant's responses. Also, you must decide whether you will distribute the questionnaire in person to the participants or mail it to them or prepare it for online completion.

Complete the following questions. Some may not apply to you depending on the method of administration you choose. Simply skip those questions and go to the next set.

Note that you do not need a signed consent form for completion of an anonymous survey. But you do need a cover letter or at least an introduction covering the points above.

If the questionnaire is to be self-administered (as opposed to completed by an interviewer) and distributed by the researcher or an assistant (as opposed to online or distributed by mail):

1) When, where, and how will the questionnaire be distributed? By whom? Will it be distributed to individuals or groups? Justify your choices.

2) List the information that the person who distributes the questionnaire will give to the participant, including the following: a persuasive introduction regarding importance and purpose of the study; who is sponsoring the research; how the sample was selected (which should answer the respondents' potential questions of "Why was I selected?" and "How did you get my name?"); a statement that participation is voluntary and will not affect services for which the participant is eligible; assurance of anonymity or confidentiality; the estimated time for completion of the questionnaire; and directions for return of the questionnaire.

3) Will the questionnaire be anonymous or confidential? Include your rationale for the option you have chosen.

4) What are the conditions for questionnaire completion and return? Completed on the spot or returned later? If later, how will participants be instructed to return the

SURVEY RESEARCH

questionnaires? What is the final date for returning the questionnaires? What is your plan for follow-up of unreturned questionnaires? Justify your choices.

5) What are your plans to enhance your response rate? Anticipate and list reasons people might give for not completing the questionnaire and how you plan to respond to those.

6) Describe any compensation to the participants for their time and expenses and the procedure for compensation. (Federal rules on research stipulate that you cannot

65

offer incentives to participants, but you can compensate them for their time and other expenses they incur such as travel and child care.)

7) What are your procedures for handling a situation where an individual starts but does not complete the questionnaire?

8) What will be your process for reviewing a questionnaire for missed responses by the participant?

Now proceed to Section D.

If the questionnaire is to be self-administered and distributed by mail or online:

1) Will the questionnaire be anonymous or confidential? Include your rationale for the option you have chosen.

2) Outline a cover letter including the following: a persuasive introduction regarding importance and purpose of the study; who is sponsoring the research; how the sample was selected (which should answer the respondents' potential questions of "Why was I selected?" and "How did you get my name?"); a statement that participation is voluntary and will not affect services for which the participant is eligible; assurance of anonymity or confidentiality; the estimated time for completion of the questionnaire; directions for return of the questionnaire and the cutoff date for return of the questionnaire.

   Remember to keep your letter short and clear. Consider using bullet points. Sentences should be free of jargon and short in length. Aim for a seventh grade reading level for your consent form.

3) Indicate whether you plan to use stamped return envelopes or business reply envelopes and why.

4) Indicate your plans and dates regarding follow-up mailings, if any. What is the estimated total cost for your mailing?

5) Describe any compensation to the participants for their time and expenses and the procedure for compensation. (Federal rules on research stipulate that you cannot offer incentives to participants, but you can compensate them for their time and other expenses such as travel and child care.)

Now proceed to Section D.

If the questionnaire will be completed by an interviewer:

1) When and where will the interviews be conducted? By whom?

2) List the information that the interviewer will give to the participant prior to starting the interview, including the following: a persuasive introduction regarding importance and purpose of the study; who is sponsoring the research; how the sample was selected (which should answer the respondents' potential questions of "Why was I selected?" and "How did you get my name?"); a statement that participation is voluntary and will not affect services for which the participant is eligible; assurance of anonymity or confidentiality; and the estimated time for completion of the interview.

3) What are your plans to enhance your response rate; i.e., to persuade people to agree to be interviewed? Anticipate and list some reasons people might give for not completing the questionnaire and how you plan to respond to those.

4) Describe any compensation to the participants for their time and expenses and the procedure for compensation. (Federal rules on research stipulate that you cannot offer incentives to participants, but you can compensate them for their time and other expenses they incur, such as travel and child care.)

5) What are your procedures for handling a situation where an individual starts but does not complete the interview?

D. PILOT YOUR RESEARCH INSTRUMENT AND PLAN FOR DATA COLLECTION

The validity and reliability of your questionnaire can be greatly enhanced by piloting it prior to your actual data collection. This also helps you anticipate any problems related to administration. *You must obtain approval from the IRB and agency personnel before piloting your interview with clients.*

1) Pilot your instrument, making conditions as similar as possible to those you expect during data collection. Enlist people who are similar to those in your intended study population, perhaps clients of the agency who would not eventually receive the questionnaire.   Indicate with whom you piloted your instrument and the results of the pilots. Discuss questions that were problematic for people, variations in length of time to administer, logistical problems regarding where and how the interviews were conducted, and any problems with administering the consent form.

2) Indicate the changes you will make in the administration of your study based on the results of your pilot.

3) Revise your questionnaire and have your course instructor and field instructor approve the final version. And keep this sage observation in mind as you go forth with your final version: The *next* version of your questionnaire will be the *best* version.

E.   WRITE THE METHODS SECTION

Again, this will be a first draft of this section of your paper. As you proceed through the following steps, you may return to this section and make revisions. This section will vary in length according to how many measures you have chosen. You can expect this section of the paper to be roughly two to three pages. It should include the following information:

- Each major variable, starting with the dependent variable, if applicable
- The chosen measure(s) for each variable, and if applicable, how they were used in prior studies
- Validity and reliability of each measure
- A brief overview of pilot efforts
- Details of plans for administration of the questionnaire
- Consent procedures and protection of data.

F.   DATA COLLECTION

Data collection should follow the plan you set out in this section. Once you have completed data collection, you will revise the methods section to report how you actually collected the data.

CHAPTER 7

QUALITATIVE RESEARCH

RECOMMENDED ARTICLE:
Siegel, D. H. (2003). Open adoption of infants: Adoptive parents' feelings seven years later. *Social Work, 48*(3), 409-419.

The goal of qualitative research is to study a problem in-depth from the perspective of the research participants in order to understand the meanings people give to situations and experiences. In qualitative research the data are text rather than numbers.

Qualitative studies are similar to social work case studies and seek to understand what people believe and feel about a particular problem, situation, or program. Social workers often find qualitative research interviewing to be similar to interviewing clients in practice. The goals, however, are different. In practice, our goal is to help clients with their problems and concerns. In qualitative research, our goal is to obtain information that can help us answer our research question.

Qualitative studies help us understand a problem or situation by focusing on a small number of people's experiences. Program evaluations, needs assessments, and client satisfaction studies can be conducted using qualitative methods as well. Data for qualitative studies are most often collected through interviewing, by observation, and from existing documents such as agency documents and newspaper articles. Although there are several methods for collecting qualitative data, we focus solely on structured or semi-structured interviewing with individuals or groups. Structured and semi-structured interviews both have specific open-ended questions that are asked of each participant. This format permits comparisons among the participants and data that are easier to analyze than data from unstructured interviews. Unstructured qualitative interviews should be left to experienced researchers.

Qualitative methods are not easier than quantitative methods just because you don't have to "do" statistics. After completing the interviews, the researcher must analyze and synthesize text data rather than numeric data. There are several qualitative analysis software programs available that can assist with the process of your data analysis. On their web page, the American Evaluation Association describes various software programs http://www.eval.org/Resources/QDA.htm). You may also want to see if your university has qualitative analysis software that you can use. However, computer programs will not do the thinking for you. Qualitative analysis requires rigorous analytical thinking and the ability to

73

convey that in written form. Keep in mind that the perspectives of the research participants are of utmost importance and relevance to a qualitative study.

REMINDER:

Review a text devoted to qualitative methods. A general research text may not provide enough information to help you conduct a good qualitative study.

A. DEVELOP THE INTERVIEW AGENDA

Begin by reviewing your research question and your rationale for deciding to conduct a qualitative study. Qualitative research questions are generally not as precise as quantitative questions. However, you must have a good understanding of your topic, the focus of your study, and who your research participants will be. The section on *nonprobability samples* in Chapter 10, Sample Design, will help you plan how you will select your sample. Qualitative methods texts present more detailed information that will help you select a sample and develop your interview agenda.

1) Develop a list of demographic and other general information you want to collect for each participant, such as age, race, gender, marital/partner status, education, employment, or income.

2) Refer to your literature review to remind yourself what others studying your topic have found. List the specific topics they included in their studies.

3) Now, generate a list of the topics that relate directly to your research question. Use what you learned from the literature review and your own personal experiences with the population and area you are studying. Stay focused on your research question. There will by many areas related to your topic, but you will not have time to explore them all. List the general topics you want to cover.

4) Ask your field instructor, other agency staff, clients, and your peers for their suggestions regarding topics to include in the interviews. List to whom you talked and their suggestions.

5) From your research topics, develop eight to ten open-ended questions on a separate page. These questions should solicit information intended to answer your research question. Don't worry about the order of the questions at this point, but you should pay special attention to the wording. Questions should be focused, yet broad enough to allow the participants to share their perspectives. Avoid biases of age; race; gender; social class; physical, mental, or emotional ability; or sexual orientation.

6) Now, add key points that you want to cover under each of the main questions that you have developed. These points will provide guidance for the interviewer (even if you are the only interviewer) and ensure that you ask the same questions of all participants.

7) Draft your interview agenda on separate pages, putting your questions and key points under each one, in a format that follows a logical order. Questions should move from general to specific and from less sensitive to more sensitive topics. The interview format should make sense to your participants *and* allow you to stay focused while collecting data.

Circulate the draft of your interview agenda to the people who helped you generate questions and to other individuals as well. Obtain their feedback and revise your interview agenda. List with whom you talked and the feedback they gave.

B.   PLAN HOW TO CONDUCT INTERVIEWS

REMINDER:
> Refer to a qualitative methods text for information about conducting in-depth interviews with individuals or in a group setting (focus groups).

1) Indicate whether you will conduct individual or group interviews. Give the rationale for your choice. When conducting group interviews, remind yourself to hear from each participant and don't expect agreement among participants.

2) How and where will the interviews be scheduled? Locate a quiet, comfortable place in which you can avoid interruptions and that allows for confidentiality.

3) There are various methods for collecting qualitative data. Tape recording with a digital audio recorder and having your interviews transcribed verbatim is one method. However, you may not have the resources for this. (One hour of interview time takes at least three to four hours to transcribe and can result in 30 pages or more of typed data.) Voice recognition software may assist with this task; see a review of different software programs at http://www.consumersearch.com/www/ software/voice-recognition-software.

Other means of recording qualitative interview data include: 1) taping with partial transcribing, 2) taping and later taking notes while listening to the tapes, and 3) taking extensive notes during and after the interviews when recording is not possible. It is helpful to include another person as note taker so you can focus on the interview. Notes taken before, during, and after the interviews are commonly referred to as field notes.

What will you need to conduct the interview? How will you record the data?

4) Indicate who will conduct the interviews. If there is more than one interviewer, how will you prepare the interviewers so that the interviews are conducted consistently? Specify the training and supervision interviewers will receive.

5) Describe any compensation to the participants for their time and expenses and the procedure for compensation. (Federal rules on research stipulate that you cannot offer incentives to participants, but you can compensate them for their time and other expenses they incur such as travel and child care.)

6) List the information you will give to the participant just prior to the start of the interview, including the following: a persuasive introduction regarding importance and purpose of the study; who is sponsoring the research; how the sample was selected (which should answer the respondents' potential questions of "Why was I selected?" and "How did you get my name?"); a statement that participation is voluntary and will not affect services for which the participant is eligible; assurance of anonymity or confidentiality; the estimated time for completion of the interview; and how the data will be recorded. Remember to also have the participant read and sign the consent form prior to the interview.

On a separate page, write the information into a script that the interviewer can read to participants before beginning the interviews.

7) What are your procedures for handling a situation where an individual starts but does not complete the interview?

8) Indicate your plan for handling a situation in which an individual becomes upset during the interview.

C. PILOT YOUR INTERVIEW AGENDA AND PLAN FOR DATA COLLECTION

Piloting your interview can help you identify and remedy potential problems in data collection. *You must obtain approval from IRB and agency personnel before piloting your interview with clients.* Coordinate this through your course instructor and field instructor.

1) Pilot your interview agenda, making conditions as similar as possible to those you expect during data collection. You may interview agency staff, classmates, or clients who would not eventually be interviewed for your study. Indicate with whom you piloted the interview and how long the interview took; include their feedback. Add your own ideas regarding what you think worked well and what you would like to change.

2) Revise your interview agenda using your experience and the feedback from participants with whom you piloted the instrument. Obtain final approval of the interview agenda from your field instructor and course instructor.

D. WRITE THE METHODS SECTION

In the first draft of this section (roughly two to three pages), you should include the following:

- How you developed the interview agenda
- Whether you will conduct individual or group interviews
- How you plan to record the data
- Who will conduct the interviews and how they will be trained
- Results of your pilot efforts
- Consent procedures and protection of data

E. DATA COLLECTION

Data collection should follow the plan you set out in this section. Once you have completed data collection, you will revise the methods section to report how you actually collected the data.

NOTES:

CHAPTER 8

SINGLE-CASE DESIGN

RECOMMENDED ARTICLE:

Brophy, G. (2000). Social work treatment of sleep disturbance in a 5-year-old boy: A single-case evaluation. *Research on Social Work Practice, (10)*6, 749-760.

Single-case design is also referred to as single-*system* design, reflecting its applicability to any client system—a single individual, a single family, a single program, a single community. We assume that most students using this design will choose a single individual as the client system. We have developed the material with that in mind. It is not difficult, however, to adapt and complete this chapter with a different client system in mind, and we encourage you not to overlook other client systems when considering your options.

Single-case research is a frequently utilized method of evaluating one's practice. Its implementation parallels many of the activities of good practice. It allows you to evaluate your practice while at the same time it provides a system for ongoing feedback to both you and your client on how well your work is progressing. Single-case design requires the selection of measures that can be collected frequently (daily or weekly at least) so that you can record and visually examine progress on a graph.

Single-case design is inherently a causal study asking whether an intervention is effective. To what extent does the intervention cause a change in the client? As such, it requires the researcher to be aware of the internal and external validity limitations of the design. We encourage you to review this aspect of single-case design as you plan your study.

This chapter of the workbook is intended to guide you through the steps of designing a single-case study. First you must determine whether your client is willing to participate in your research study. Review a copy of the consent form with the client. (The consent form is developed in Chapter 11.) Be sure that your client does not feel pressured to participate and understands that refusal to participate will not affect receipt of or eligibility for agency services.

A. TRANSLATE CONCEPTS INTO VARIABLES

REMINDER:
Review single-case design and operationalization and measurement in a methods text.

In your literature review you identified major concepts and variables from other studies and indicated the measures (indicators) chosen for each of them. Now you will specify the indicators for each variable you intend to measure.

In single-case design studies, the dependent variable is the target goal chosen by the client and worker. These target goals should be reflected in the case plan that you have developed with the client. One of the advantages of a single-case design is that it can be tied directly to and strengthen the case plan. As you complete these steps, you may find yourself returning to the case plan and making changes that will clarify what you and your client are working on. What are the goals that your client is interested in pursuing? Your literature review should reflect material on your goals. Keep in mind that more than one target goal may be chosen.

List two or three goals (variables or outcome measures) that you and your client have chosen.

B. TRANSLATE VARIABLES INTO MEASURES (OPERATIONALIZATION)

There are three broad categories of sources for finding measures: questions or scales currently used by the agency, questions or scales you find in the literature, and your own creations. One advantage of the literature review you did earlier is that it will give you a sense of how others have defined and measured outcomes relative to the issues your intervention addresses.

The important issue in single-case design is that you select measures that will reveal changes over short periods of time. There are some obvious measures that easily meet these criteria such as number of classes missed each day, number of tantrums per day, number of days attending school per week. If these measures fit for your chosen goals, they will work well for a single-case design. However, sometimes you will need to use less obvious measures. For example, perhaps you want to evaluate your work on reducing a child's overall level of aggression in his interactions with peers, and it is not feasible for school personnel to keep track of his interactions on a daily basis.

In the literature you might find an evaluation of an intervention designed to reduce aggressive behavior in elementary school youth. Perhaps the school social worker conducted a nine-week group for targeted youth, and the researchers found that at posttest the youth scored better on an aggression scale as compared to their baseline scores. You might decide that the aggression scale is perfect for your purposes. However, if your study is a single-case design, what you must first determine is whether the scale is sensitive enough to show change over a short period of time. You would want to be able to administer the scale weekly to your client and put the scale score on a graph showing progress from week to week. You would have to do further research on the scale to determine if it would fit that criterion.

In the case of scales that are used in studies and cited in articles, you may have to locate the article that contains the actual items of the scale and includes information about the development and testing of that scale. The article will be listed in the references of the study article you have read. Sometimes you may need to call or write the author to see the actual scale. Some scales are copyrighted and can be used only if a fee is paid for their use. If you plan to use an existing scale, allow time to find these things out and obtain a copy of the scale.

There are also texts which include many scales such as Fischer and Corcoran's (2006) *Measures for Clinical Practice* and Jordan and Franklin's (2003) *Clinical Assessment for*

Social Workers. These usually can be found in your library's reference section. For additional suggestions see Rubin and Babbie's (2008) *Research Methods for Social Work*.

Finally, in addition to the other resources available, don't overlook your agency's resources. They may have instruments that are available for your use. If, on the other hand, you develop your own instrumentation, allow time to share it with others and receive feedback.

1) What are the dependent variables (outcomes) you are considering? Drawing from your literature review, how have others measured each of these?

   On the following page, specify each variable, then complete the information in the table. If the agency has measured these variables before, include their measures or questions.

2) Your intended measures:

   a) Circle the measures that you plan to use. Relative to scales, indicate how much time it will take to complete the scale, either by interview, observation, or self-administered. If you do not plan to use any of the reviewed measures, or you plan to add measures of your own, continue to Part b; otherwise go to Part d.

   b) If none of the above measures seems appropriate, or if you want to develop measures of your own in addition to conventional measures you have selected, indicate why and the measures you propose.

VARIABLE AUTHOR & DATE	MEASURE	BRIEF DESCRIPTION	SCALE RELIABILITY & VALIDITY	HOW COLLECTED & TIME INVOLVED
1)				
2)				
3)				

c) Don't assume that because a scale is cited often or copyrighted, it is bias-free. Evaluate whether your chosen measures have a cultural bias in terms of age; race; gender; social class; physical, mental or emotional ability; or sexual orientation. In the case of validated scales, with whom and with what age group have the scales been tested for validity and reliability?

d) Discuss potential limitations of your measures relative to reliability and validity.

3) Other considerations for your measures:

a) Regardless of the measure(s) you have chosen, what will be your data source? Some of your options include using available records, doing interviews, direct observation, and self-reporting (including the use of logs and journals).

b) Who will be responsible for collecting the data? What is the potential for reactivity, obtrusiveness, and social desirability biases?

c) Consider each of the following questions to finalize your choice of measures:

   ✓ To what extent are the measures sensitive to small, short-term changes?
   ✓ Are or can the indicators be phrased positively?
   ✓ For the target goals, will you measure frequency, duration, magnitude, or a combination?

4) Indicate how you will triangulate the target goal measures.

5) Specify what your intervention will be (location, specific activities, duration, frequency).

C. IDENTIFY THE SPECIFIC SINGLE-CASE DESIGN

Your choice of design will depend on what is practical in your agency and with your client, the nature of the intervention (varying intensity, multiple components, irreversible effects) and the chosen target goals. At a minimum, you should use an AB design, expanding on it as possible.

1) Sketch out a simple graph of an AB design. Mark the X-axis with the range of scores for the selected target goal and the Y-axis with the intended observation points. Draw a vertical line across the Y-axis at the point where you intend to begin the intervention, demarcating the baseline and intervention phases.

2) Evaluate your design with attention to these questions.

   a) Baseline phase:
      ✓ Do you have enough measurement points that a stable baseline can be established (five to ten points)?
      ✓ If it is not feasible to collect baseline date, how can you use retrospective data for construction of the baseline?
      ✓ Can you use multiple baselines, either for different target goals or with different clients?

   b) Intervention phase:
      ✓ Do you intend to withdraw the intervention for some period of time and then provide it again (an ABAB design)? Indicate when and how on the graph.
      ✓ Do you have an intervention that will be offered in changing intensity (an $AB^1B^2B^3$ design)? Explain and add to the graph.
      ✓ Do you have an intervention with several components (an ABCD design)? Specify on your graph.

3) Would it be possible to do more than one single-case study; i.e., use the same

design with more than one client? Explain how this could strengthen your study.

4) Indicate the limitations relative to internal validity. (See pages 119-120 for a review of threats to internal validity.)

5) Indicate the limitations relative to external validity.

D.   WRITE THE METHODS SECTION

Again, this will be a first draft of this section because, as you proceed through the other steps, you may return and make revisions. This section will vary in length (roughly one to two pages) according to how many measures you have chosen. It should include the following information:

- Dependent variables (the target goals) and the client's input
- The chosen measure(s) for each variable and their use in prior studies
- The validity and reliability of each measure
- The independent variable (the intervention)
- Details on the chosen design, rationale, and limitations
- Consent form and protection of data

E. DATA COLLECTION

Data collection should follow the plan you set out in this section. Once you have completed data collection, you will revise the methods section to report how you actually collected the data.

NOTE:

Because single-case designs use an "N of 1," you do not need to complete Chapter 10 of the workbook (Sample Design), and you should disregard references to the sample when writing the final report in Chapter 15. You should, however, give a brief synopsis of the client situation and the circumstances that led to their choice of goals. Proceed to Chapter 14.

CHAPTER 9

OUTCOME EVALUATION

RECOMMENDED ARTICLES:

Michalski, J. H., Mishna, F., Worthington, C., & Cummings, R. (2003). A multi-method impact evaluation of a therapeutic summer camp program. *Child and Adolescent Social Work Journal, (20)*1, 53-76.

Mulroy, E. A. & Lauber, H. (2004). A user-friendly approach to program evaluation and effective community interventions for families at risk of homelessness. *Social Work, (49)*4, 573-586.

Another field of research is called program evaluation, of which there are several types. Process evaluation and outcome evaluation are the two most common types of program evaluation.

Funders will often require a *process* evaluation as part of a funding agreement. While we do not provide a chapter on process evaluation in this workbook, we mention it here to clarify how it fits with program evaluation and because we want to point out its usefulness as a research product.

A process evaluation may precede or occur simultaneously with an outcome evaluation. The focus of a process evaluation is on how the agency implements a program and/or evaluation. Imagine you read great things about a program that is meeting the needs of the same population that your agency serves and you want to start a similar program. What is the most useful information you could obtain? Probably answers to questions such as: *What exactly did they do? What staffing and training did they have? What was it that worked well? What problems did they encounter? What did they fail to anticipate when they started? How did they handle the challenges of getting the program up and running? What would they recommend to others?* That is a process evaluation. Another way to conceive of a process evaluation is to imagine a reporter chronicling the development and implementation of a program from day one through implementation.

Outcome evaluation is another type of program evaluation. Some researchers make a distinction between outcome *evaluation* and outcome *monitoring*. In both types, we are interested in specifying the intended outcomes of a program. In outcome monitoring, the focus is on tracking the outcome results over time. In outcome evaluation, the focus is on demonstrating that the intervention is responsible for achieving the intended outcomes.

An outcome monitoring project is often chosen rather than an outcome evaluation because a program is new or an agency is just beginning to conduct research. Staff members do well to start small and with something manageable. In other instances, it may be impractical or too difficult to develop the control or comparison group that is required for comparing people receiving the intervention to those not receiving it (outcome *evaluation*). Only with a control or comparison group can you determine if the changes found are the result of your program. You will be able to use this chapter of the workbook for either an outcome monitoring study or an outcome evaluation study.

We want to emphasize that outcome evaluation is as much about the process as it is the final report, perhaps moreso. What is learned in the course of doing an outcome evaluation can sometimes provide more useful information than the outcome data itself. For example, when reviewing data collection efforts by staff, one can uncover inconsistencies in how instruments are administered or differing opinions on what goals are acceptable in a treatment plan or even what constitutes successful completion of a goal. As findings are reviewed, questions will often arise about the cultural appropriateness of particular scales or the timeframe within which progress is expected to be seen. These revelations, questions, and debates are indicators of a successful evaluation. They demonstrate that staff members are engaged in reflective practice, and that they are making the connection between program and outcome. Every outcome evaluation should have a feedback loop so that information about both the process and the outcome is discussed by the staff providing the intervention. Keep in mind: the ultimate goal of any evaluation is program improvement.

You may remember from your research methods class a research design called the *one group pretest-posttest design*. We will discuss design issues in more detail in Section C, but for now we want to note that the *one group pretest-posttest design* is the type of design used in an outcome monitoring study. Outcomes are measured at baseline and follow-up for one group of clients. This allows you to determine if changes in the outcome measures have occurred. You will not be able to claim, however, that the program was responsible for the change. It does not provide evidence of the program as a factor in that change, since, without comparative data from a comparison group, any number of factors might account for the change.

The United Way has developed an excellent resource for agencies to use when engaging in outcome evaluation. The manual is simple, basic, and geared to beginners. It contains many examples of outcome statements and outcome measures applied to several different types of programs. We encourage you to examine *Measuring Program Outcomes: A Practical Approach* (1996), often available through your local United Way or by calling Sales Service/America at 800-772-0008 and asking for item number 0989. You can also check with your library to see if they have a copy.

LOGIC MODELS

Evaluating the extent to which a program or intervention causes the intended outcome has become increasingly important as more funding sources require outcome evaluations. However, outcome evaluation has its own intrinsic rewards. Programs can benefit simply from the process of designing an evaluation when providers take the time to consider the "match" between their services and the intended outcomes. *What can we realistically expect to happen as a result of this program?* This is often referred to as the logic or rationale behind a program. Evaluators will sometimes speak in terms of a "logic model."

There are a variety of ways one can construct a logic model. The one you choose is dependent upon your purpose. Do you want to emphasize the assumptions that underlie your program? For example, in a program to reduce recidivism among juvenile offenders, what is the rationale (logic) for exactly how the intervention is expected to impact the teen? One could posit that by providing role models with whom the teen can identify, he or she will seek to emulate that person rather than other delinquent peers. Or perhaps the program is based on giving teens work and training opportunities so that they have less time to become involved in delinquent activity. Whatever the basis for the program, a *theory-based logic model* will outline how the program is designed according to those assumptions.

An *implementation-based logic model*, however, focuses more on the activities of the program, similar in some respects to the kind of information gathered for a process evaluation. Such a model would outline the specific steps for carrying out the program as designed and will often include "milestone markers," specific program targets to be achieved along the way. This might include, for example, composition of an interagency coordinating committee, development of a manual detailing program design, development of the data to be collected and the collection process, plans for staff training, initial implementation in a single unit, roll-out to the entire agency, etc.

An *outcomes-based logic model* represents yet another type. This is the type of model used in the United Way guide mentioned above. It places emphasis on the specific outcomes chosen in a program evaluation, sometimes dividing them into short-term, intermediate, and long-term outcomes. Oftentimes the specific measures for each outcome will be indicated.

Which logic model you choose is less important than designing a model that meets your particular needs. In some instances staff members need clarity about why and how their particular activities are supposed to result in the desired ends. In other instances staff members need a roadmap for program implementation. You should create a logic model that fits your purpose. It may include elements of all three types mentioned above. But be careful that the model does not become so complex that it is not easily understood. Think of the logic model as a graphic display of whatever it is you want to emphasize, a picture that speaks for itself rather than one which needs a tour guide to interpret it.

Lastly, do not overlook the value of a logic model as a tool not only for program evaluation but also for program design. Clarity about how program and outcome are linked to each other is the first step towards effective practice.

Consider this example. The objectives for a therapeutic arts program in a juvenile detention facility include the reduction of aggressive behaviors, and in the long run, a lower rate of recidivism. But should an arts program meeting two hours a week for ten weeks be expected to have these results? The program directors realized that such limited exposure in the context of so many influences in a teen's life was unlikely to have a major impact on whether the teen committed future delinquent offenses. Further, as the program directors explained the rationale behind their program, they fully expected that the program, if successful, might initially *increase* acting out behaviors of youth as they began to confront issues in their lives. Simply the *process* of designing an evaluation of their program was helpful to the program directors as they thought through the rationale (logic) behind their intervention and what they sought to accomplish (outcomes) with it. For the purposes of this chapter we use a logic model that specifies both assumptions and outcomes.

- In Section A we will guide you through the process of specifying the *logic model* behind your intervention. Laying out the rationale or logic for an intervention and clarifying the link between the intervention and the program's objectives or goals will answer the question of *why* staff members expect clients to change as a result of receiving the intervention.
- The next task in an outcome evaluation is to specify the *program outcomes and their measures* (Section B). Sometimes programs have stated objectives that lend themselves to the development of outcome measures. Other times, when the objectives are more general or unwritten, the development of outcome measures takes more thought. We guide you through the various steps for constructing solid outcome measures.
- The third task in designing your study is the development of a plan for when and how the data will be collected. We refer you to Chapter 6, Survey Research, where we provide a series of questions to help you incorporate the necessary considerations for specifying your *data collection procedures*.
- The fourth task involves developing how you can demonstrate that the observed change is a result of the intervention and not other factors in the clients' lives—internal validity (Section C). This is the task of *research design,* and we provide two different designs commonly used to evaluate programs (comparison group design and control group design) and guide you through the process of choosing one.
- The fifth task is to specify your sample design (Section D).
- The final task is to identify threats to the internal validity of your study (Section E).

At the end of this chapter we provide an example of a logic model in an outcome evaluation of the Quest Program, a program designed to improve adherence to a medication regimen. You may find it helpful to review the example before continuing on in this chapter, and then once again after reviewing the material in this chapter.

A.   DEVELOPING THE RATIONALE FOR THE INTERVENTION: A LOGIC MODEL

1) Specify what your program is supposed to do. Describe the program in terms of targeted problems, services delivered (type, frequency, and duration), who provides the services, and where the services are provided. Provide a thorough but succinct description in one (albeit long) sentence. This will clarify the specific program components that you expect to facilitate change for your clients.

2) What are the stated goals or outcomes of the program? (Goals and outcomes are not necessarily the same thing. We will clarify the distinction in a later step. For now, state in general terms what the program is trying to accomplish.) The goals may be written in program literature (brochures, reports for funding sources, grants) or they may not be written, in which case you will need to seek clarification from agency staff.

3) Explain the rationale linking the intervention with the goals you have identified. Another way to think of this is to imagine you are explaining to a friend how and why the intervention or program *should* accomplish the goals of the program.

B. DEVELOPING PROGRAM OUTCOMES AND THEIR MEASURES

REMINDER:
Review your methods text regarding operationalization and measurement.

If you have ever been confused about the distinction between goals, objectives, targets, benchmarks, outcomes, measures, and indicators, rest assured you are not alone. Because there is no commonly accepted set of definitions for these terms, it is one of the most confusing areas in evaluation research. If one of the tasks in learning to do research can be likened to learning a foreign language, evaluation research is even more difficult because not everyone is speaking the same language. How the terms are defined and used varies from author to author.

Our advice is this: If you are writing a grant proposal or providing a project report to a funding source, use their definitions. If they do not provide any, determine if they have specific definitions in mind. If not, either use the terms you already know or use ours. We provide these simple definitions and examples.

Goals are broad general statements about the desired results of a program.

- Program Goal: To improve social skills

Outcomes are more specific statements about what the program intends to accomplish, what *change* it hopes to achieve. (Objectives can often serve as outcome statements as well. Sometimes people will use "Impact Statement" to refer to an outcome.)

- Program Outcome (Objective): To reduce the number of aggressive incidents in the group home and at school

When developing outcomes, keep in mind that the outcome must indicate change—in knowledge, attitudes, behavior, condition, or status (e.g., from danger to safety in housing condition). If the outcome does not indicate change, it is probably what others refer to as an *output* or a *product* of the program. Agencies generally measure outputs such as number of clients served, hours of service provided, and/or client satisfaction. These are *not* outcomes. (An exception to this would be programs that provide emergency services only, such as shelters, food pantries, and meal programs. The intended outcome in this instance is the commodity provided; the program does not seek to facilitate change in the client.) For good measure, we repeat: client satisfaction measures are *not* outcome measures.

Indicators or measures are the specific data items that are used to determine if the outcomes (or objectives) have been accomplished.

- Program Measure: Number of incident reports

Targets are simply that, targets for the outcome to achieve.

- Program Target: To have 20 or fewer incident reports in the next quarter

Benchmarks are another type of target, one to beat. People may use last year's measure or a measure from a similar program.

- Program Benchmark: We will have 50% fewer incidents per quarter this year as compared to the previous year.
- Program Benchmark: We will be at or below the average incident rate for similar facilities in all of Region V.

The following steps will guide you through the process of specifying your outcomes. There may be more than one outcome, and the outcomes may be linked to each other. For example, an increase in *knowledge* about HIV/AIDS promotes safer sex *behavior* (further defined as condom use) which in term leads to a reduction in the rate of infection in a community (*condition*). A program may seek to accomplish all of those outcomes; however, for the purposes of your study, you might select only two of them for evaluation, depending upon your purpose, time, and money available for the study.

1) If this is your first study, keep it simple: choose two or three outcomes to measure. The outcomes may already be identified in the program literature. If not, you will need to develop the specific outcome statements for your program. Use this checklist to evaluate and strengthen your outcome statements.

   Outcome statements:

   ✓ Reflect change in client behavior, skills, attitudes, knowledge, or condition.
   ✓ Follow logically from what the program is trying to accomplish, with all stakeholders in agreement (clients, staff, funders).
   ✓ Are reasonable expectations for measurable change within the timeframe of the study.

   Specify your outcomes.

2) Once you have identified the intended program outcomes, the next step is to specify how to measure your outcomes. How will you know if the intended changes occurred? What evidence will you have that indicates change?

There are three broad categories of sources for finding measures: 1) questions or scales currently used by the agency, 2) questions or scales you find in the literature, and 3) your own creations. One advantage of the literature review you conducted earlier is that you have a sense of how others have defined and measured outcomes relative to the issues your intervention addresses.

In the case of scales used in studies and cited in articles, you may have to locate another article that contains the actual items of the scale and includes information about the development and testing of that scale. Check the references for the original article. You may call or write the author to see the actual scale and gain permission to use it. Some scales are copyrighted and a fee is charged for their use. If you plan to use an existing scale, allow time to obtain permission to use the scale.

In addition to scales and measures found in your literature review, your agency may also have instruments that are available for your use. Also, check for texts that include multiple scales such as Fischer and Corcoran's (2006) *Measures for Clinical Practice* and Jordan and Franklin's (2003) *Clinical Assessment for Social Workers*. These usually can be found in your library's reference section. For additional suggestions see Rubin and Babbie's (2008) *Research Methods for Social Work*.

If, on the other hand, you develop your own measurement instrument, allow time to share it with others and receive feedback.

What are the dependent variables (outcomes) you are considering? Drawing from your literature review, how have others measured each outcome variable?

On the following page, specify each variable, then complete the information in the table. If the agency has measured these variables before, include their measures or questions.

VARIABLE AUTHOR & DATE	MEASURE	BRIEF DESCRIPTION	SCALE RELIABILITY & VALIDITY	HOW COLLECTED & TIME INVOLVED
1)				
2)				
3)				

3) Your intended measures:

    a) Circle the measures that you plan to use. Relative to scales, indicate how much
        time it will take to complete the scale, either by interview or self-administered.
        If you do not plan to use any of the reviewed measures, continue to Part b;
        otherwise go to Part d.

    b) If none of the above measures seems appropriate, or if you want to develop
        measures of your own in addition to conventional measures you have selected,
        indicate why.

c) What measure(s) do you propose?

d) Don't assume that because a scale is cited often or copyrighted, that it is bias-free. Evaluate whether your chosen measures have a cultural bias in terms of age; race; gender; social class; physical, mental or emotional ability; or sexual orientation.

e) In the case of validated scales, with whom and with what age group have the scales been tested for validity and reliability?

f) Discuss potential limitations of your measures relative to reliability and validity.

Now you are ready to construct your research questionnaire and develop a plan for administering it. Turn to Chapter 6, Survey Research, complete Sections B, C, and D, and then return here.

C. CHOOSING A DESIGN

Once you have specified your outcomes and measures, constructed your research instrument, and specified your plan for data collection, you are ready to choose your research design. The following questions will help you determine which design you will be able to use.

1) Can you *randomly assign* some participants to a group that will receive your intervention and others to either a group that will receive an alternative treatment (actually comparing the relative effectiveness of the two treatments) or to a waiting list group who will receive the treatment after the first group has finished the program?

   If yes, then you can conduct a *control group design*, a true experimental design. Consult your research methods text for a review of that design and proceed to Part 4. Otherwise, continue to the next question.

2) Is there a group that is similar to the group of individuals receiving your intervention? Can you gather the same information from this group over the same period of time as your treatment group?

   If yes, then you can conduct a *comparison group design*, sometimes also called a *nonequivalent control group design*, a quasi-experimental design. Consult your research methods text for a review of that design and proceed to Part 4. Otherwise, continue to the next question.

3) If you cannot do either of the above, your last alternative is to conduct a *one group pretest-posttest design*. You will obtain baseline measures for participants prior to the intervention and then again at completion of the intervention. Consult your research methods text for a review of that design.

   Keep in mind that a *one group pretest-posttest design* offers virtually no internal validity and thus does not provide evidence that the observed changes are a result of your intervention. *One group pretest-posttest designs* serve primarily for outcome monitoring. Often, given the constraints of time and resources, this design is the only feasible one. It is of value nonetheless as it still requires specification of the link between intervention and objectives, development of outcome measures, and a plan for data collection.

4) Draw a diagram of your study design, using standard notation for group designs.

D.   SELECTING A SAMPLE AND ASSIGNING GROUPS

Students often confuse *random selection* (which has to do with *sample* selection) with *random assignment* (which has to do with how a treatment and control group are formed *after* a sample has been selected). That is why we present it as *selecting* a sample and *assigning* groups.

Regardless of which design you are using, you must decide how you will select your sample of program participants. In some cases the number of program participants is small enough that you will choose to study all of them. This makes your study sample the same as your study population, the group to whom you can generalize your study findings. In other cases, the number of program participants will be too large to include in your sample, and you will have to select some of them for your study. The larger group is the study *population* from which you select a study *sample*.

1) If you plan to conduct a *one group pretest-posttest design*, at this point you should complete Chapter 10, Sample Design, and then return to this chapter, Section E.

   If you plan to conduct a comparison group design, continue to Part 2.

   If you plan to conduct a control group design, skip to Part 4.

2) For a *comparison group design*, you will have two samples: those who receive the intervention and those who do not. The credibility of this design relies upon the extent to which you can demonstrate that your comparison group is similar to your treatment group. But how does one choose a group that will be comparable?

   For example, if you were to compare juvenile offenders receiving a therapeutic arts program to offenders in another facility without such a program, you would need to demonstrate that the groups were similar, but in what ways?

   One resolution to this problem is to rely on demographic characteristics as proxy measures for the comparability of the two groups. Because other characteristics are often linked to demographic differences, if you can demonstrate that your groups are similar in terms of demographics (age, race, gender, etc.), people will be willing to consider that other factors linked to your outcome are likely to be similar in the two groups.

Given these considerations, which populations do you think might provide an equivalent comparison group for your treatment group? List them and indicate how they are similar to and different from your treatment group.

3) You can show that your groups are similar on demographic variables, but that is not necessarily sufficient. In the juvenile offender example, if you found that the treatment group was better able to express anger appropriately at the end of the study as compared to the comparison group, you would not want someone to dispute your findings by noting an obvious way that the comparison group was different to begin with.

For example, if the juvenile offenders receiving treatment were at a minimum-security facility, and the juvenile offenders in the comparison group were at a maximum-security facility, one could argue that the reason the treatment group fared better on expressing anger appropriately was that they were a less violent group to begin with.

Consider any important ways your two groups might differ. To answer this question, you will draw on your knowledge of the literature relative to the factors that have been shown to influence the outcomes you intend to measure.

a) List the factors that previous studies have shown to be related to the outcomes you are studying.

b) Now ask yourself: Would any of the groups you listed in Part 2 above *obviously* differ from your treatment group on any of these characteristics? If so, it is probably not a good choice. Consider, also, that whatever group becomes your comparison group, they will need to be available for data collection of the same type and at the same times as your treatment group.

c) Now you should complete Chapter 10, Sample Design, once for your treatment group and a second time for your comparison group. Then return to Section E of this chapter.

4) If you plan to conduct a control group design, you must randomly assign the individuals in your sample to separate groups, usually a group that receives the treatment you are studying and a group that receives either an alternative treatment or a group that is placed on a waiting list to receive services at a later date.

a) Indicate whether you will use a wait list control group or alternative treatment control group. How will you randomly assign people to the two groups?

b) The assumption of random assignment is that you will have created two groups whose participants are similar to each other on all characteristics. This assumption is easily violated in small samples.

For example, imagine a sample of 20 people randomly split into two groups. The assumption is that the numbers of males and females in one group will be the same in the other group, that the age groupings in one group will be the same as those in the other group, that the variation in attitudes in one group will be just the same in the other group, and so on. However, probability theory tells us that with only 20 people in our sample, it is quite possible that the two groups will not be entirely equivalent in these areas. Thus, it is necessary to gather and present basic demographic and baseline information about the two groups to consider the extent to which they are actually similar to each other. More information on this idea of equivalency between groups is given in Parts 2 and 3 above, and you are encouraged to read it now.

On what variables can you compare your groups?

5) Complete Chapter 10, Sample Design, then return to Section E of this chapter.

E.   THREATS TO INTERNAL VALIDITY

Regardless of the design you have chosen, there will be limitations to your ability to demonstrate that the intervention is responsible for changes in your treatment group. These are known as threats to internal validity. Threats to internal validity are discussed in all research texts. Because students typically have difficulty applying these threats to particular studies, we present them at the end of the chapter in lighter fashion. Some apply only to group designs rather than single-case designs, so apply them to your study with consideration for your design type.

1) People dropping out of a study is a common and troublesome issue for researchers, so we ask you to address this threat specifically. Indicate your ideas for trying to reduce the number of *dropouts* in your study (referred to as attrition or experimental mortality).

2) For other threats to internal validity indicate each that is relevant to your study and your plan to address the threat. Depending on your design type, you may not be able to eliminate or reduce a potential threat, but you should at least recognize how it limits your conclusions.

F.   WRITE THE METHODS SECTION

This will be a first draft of this section. As you proceed through the other steps, you may return and make revisions. This section will vary in length (one to three pages) depending upon how many measures you have chosen and the complexity of your research design. It should include the following information:

- Dependent variables (the target goals) and the client's input
- The chosen measure(s) for each variable and use in prior studies
- The validity and reliability of each measure
- The independent variable (the intervention)
- How groups were formed
- Details on the chosen design, rationale, and limitations
- Consent form and protection of data.

G.   DATA COLLECTION

Data collection should follow the plan you set out in this chapter. Once you have completed data collection, you will revise the methods section to report how you actually collected the data.

LOGIC MODEL FOR THE QUEST PROGRAM

Program: QUEST
Provide bi-weekly telephone counseling to HIV+ individuals taking antiretroviral (ARV) medications.

Objectives:
1) To improve adherence to medication.
2) To improve physical health.

Logic: Recent research on adherence to ARVs suggests that adherence rates greater than 90% are necessary to maintain suppression of HIV. Numerous studies have found that rates of adherence are generally low (40%-60%) because of the difficulty people have in adapting a complex medication regimen to their daily routine. If individuals can be helped to develop ways of adapting the medication regimen to their lifestyle rather than the other way around, and if they can be supported during the time required to develop a "habit of adherence," then adherence rates should improve.

Design: Comparison group design: $\dfrac{O_1 \ x \ O_2}{O_3 \quad O_4}$

Samples:
- Experimental group: 25 randomly chosen patients from 217 outpatients at an HIV clinic at hospital X who are participants in the QUEST program.
- Comparison group: 25 randomly chosen patients from 150 outpatients at an HIV clinic at hospital Y who are receiving standard case management services.
- Experimental and comparison group are similar in that the clinics at both hospitals serve similar groups with respect to race, gender, and public vs. private pay.

Hypotheses:
1) At the end of three months, adherence will be higher for individuals who receive the intervention as compared to individuals in the comparison group.
2) At the end of three months physical health status will be better for individuals who receive the intervention as compared to individuals in the comparison group.

OUTCOMES	MEASURES	SOURCE OF DATA	WHEN COLLECTED	WHERE COLLECTED	HOW COLLECTED
Participants will demonstrate increases in adherence levels.	Number of doses taken as prescribed in each of past three days	Participant	Start of intervention (pretest) and end of intervention (posttest)	At home visit for pretest	Interview
	Number of pills left in prescription bottle on specific date compared to number that should be left	Pill count by interviewer		At home visit for posttest	Interview
Participants will have better physical health.	Lab results: CD4 counts Lab results: Viral load	Physician or Nurse (with signed consent)	Pretest and posttest	By mail	Questionnaire

INDEPENDENT VARIABLES	MEASURES	SOURCE OF DATA	WHEN COLLECTED	WHERE COLLECTED	HOW COLLECTED
Intervention	Number of phone calls completed and home visits	Social workers	Bi-weekly	Office	Case records
Race	White (not Hispanic), Afr. Am., Hispanic or Latino, Asian, Amer. Ind., Other (specify)	Participant	Pretest	Home visit	Interview
Gender	Male, Female	Participant	Pretest	Home visit	Interview
Health Insurance	Private, Medicaid, Medicare, Ryan White Funds	Participant	Pretest and posttest	Home visit	Interview
Social Support	Number of persons living with participant	Participant	Pretest and posttest	Home visit	Interview

THREATS TO INTERNAL VALIDITY

(For outcome evaluations internal validity refers to *the extent to which you are able to rule out factors other than your intervention* as explanations for your outcome findings)

The Grandma Factor

- How do we know the changes we see are a result of our efforts and not Grandma's?
- This is known as the threat of **history:** extraneous events (potentially influential) that happen at the same time as treatment.

Time Heals All Wounds

- How do we know the changes we see are a result of our efforts and not just the 6 month cycle of depression?
- How do we know the changes we see are a result of our efforts and not just the passage of time?
- This is known as the threat of **maturation** (and also, passage of time): changes over time that have nothing to do with the treatment, but nonetheless affect the results.

Practice Makes Perfect

- How do we know the changes we see are a result of our efforts and not just a result of the fact that people got a chance to practice how to answer the questions (pretest)?
- How do we know the changes we see are a result of our efforts and not just a result of the fact that people know they are being observed or that they will be measured (reactivity effect)?
- This is known as a **testing** threat to internal validity: the effect a pretest has on how people do later on some posttest treatment measure.

To Err Is Human

- How do we know the changes we see are a result of our efforts and not a result of poorly developed measures?
- How do we know the changes we see are a result of our efforts and not a function of using a different pretest and posttest that are not really equal or comparable?
- How do we know the changes we see are a result of our efforts and not a result of inconsistent ratings criteria from pretest to posttest or from one observer to another?
- This is known as an **instrumentation** threat: the effect of errors in measurement on our results.

THREATS TO INTERNAL VALIDITY

The Law of Averages

- How do we know the changes we see are a result of our efforts and do not simply reflect the fact that we got most people on a really bad day, while they were at their worst? Then at the posttest, when several of them were no longer at their worst, on average the group did better, but it had absolutely nothing to do with us.

- This is known as **statistical regression** (or regression to the mean): some change for the better will occur whenever we start with people at their worst, just because of the natural ebb and flow of struggles.

Choose Wisely

- How do we know the changes we see are a result of our efforts and not a result of simply working with people who were highly motivated to change?

- How do we know the changes we see are a result of our efforts and not a result of who we studied?

- This threat is known as a **selection bias:** the extent to which a treatment group is not comparable to a comparison or control group.

Dropouts

- How do we know the changes we see are a result of our efforts and not a function of the fact that everyone who did not benefit from our help, dropped out of the study, so our results are based only on those we did help?

- This threat to internal validity is known as **experimental mortality** or **attrition:** the rate at which people drop out of an intervention study before it is finished.

Copycat and Tattletale

What about those times when we *don't* find our help to be beneficial—the ones we work with improve, but not any more than those we didn't work with? Could something else explain that?

- Maybe those we didn't work with got the same sort of help somewhere else; from copycats, so to speak.

- Maybe those we didn't work with are chums of those we did work with, and they got all our nuggets of wisdom from their buds--tattletales, so to speak.

- This threat is known as **imitation** (copycat) or **diffusion** (tattletale) of treatment — when groups to be compared really aren't so different relative to the services they are receiving.

CHAPTER 10

SAMPLE DESIGN

REMINDER:
> Review sample design in a methods text. Pay close attention to the difference between probability and nonprobability sampling methods. Within each of those two broad types of sampling methods, review the different types of samples that can be drawn.

The first thing you must decide is whether you will select a sample based on probability or nonprobability sampling methods. This decision is dependent on several factors, including how you plan to use the information you have collected and the constraints you will face in selecting a sample (accessibility of potential participants, time, and expense).

For example, if your ultimate goal is to use data collected from a sample to make statements about a larger group of people (as in some descriptive studies), probability sampling methods will be required. However, this goal will have to be balanced against the difficulty, time, and expense of drawing a probability sample from a well-defined population. If your ultimate goal is less concerned with the generalizability of your findings and more concerned with presenting detailed information about personal experiences (as in some exploratory studies) or evaluating a program or intervention (outcome evaluation and single-case design), then you may choose to select a nonprobability sample.

Probability samples are preferred for survey methods. Single-case and outcome evaluation typically use nonprobability samples because they rely on the clients in a program rather than participants drawn from a population. Occasionally, you might be able to draw a probability sample from the clients served by the agency, in which case you should complete Section A.

Proceed to Section A if you are going to do a probability sample, Section B if nonprobability. If you are uncertain about which type of sample would work best for your study, begin with Section A on probability samples. The questions should help you determine if a probability sample is feasible for your study.

A. FOR PROBABILITY SAMPLES

1) What is the theoretical population for your study?

2) What will be your actual *study* population? (Remember, this is the group *from which* you will draw your sample. It is not the same as the theoretical population, nor is it your sample—unless you plan to study everyone in the study population.)

3) What are the screening and selection criteria for your sample?

Example: 1) at least 18 years of age, 2) with at least one child, and 3) a first time recipient of services at the agency. Be sure to specify the time frame (e.g., within the month of March). Indicate the specific procedure for sample selection.

4) What size will your sample be? Indicate your rationale and discuss the feasibility of your sample size relative to time; expense; means of contact; and level of difficulty in contact, screening, and selection.

5) Although the results from your sample are generalizable only to your study population, you are of course interested in adding to an understanding of the theoretical population. For example, since we can't study all the people who are homeless, we study some obtainable group of them, and what we learn is added to the body of knowledge about homeless people. We are thus required to discuss how our study population may differ from the theoretical population (only shelter users or only homeless people in small towns). This is helpful when trying to understand why findings from one study may differ from those of another.

In what ways will your study population differ from the theoretical population?

6) What will be the sampling frame (the actual list of potential participants) for your study population? Include the actual size of the study population or provide your best estimate. Indicate any planned safeguards for confidential information obtained in the course of constructing your sampling frame.

You will probably need to explore this with your field instructor. In some instances you might need to know confidential information about people (diagnoses, problem situations) in order to determine their inclusion in the sampling frame—for example, a study of teens identified as alcohol or drug abusers in a child welfare agency that serves all categories of children. Generally in those situations, agency personnel must first obtain client permission before releasing names to you, even though you are in placement at the agency. This is especially true in large agencies that have several divisions.

Sometimes this ethical consideration is disregarded, and it is your responsibility as an ethical researcher to ensure attention to it. To help you understand how important it is to have client consent for release of information, consider how you would feel if someone was giving to others, without your permission or knowledge, information about you, one of your children, or your parent.

Your sampling frame:

7) Consider any possible biases in your sampling frame—for example, omitted names, organization by single-service users versus multiple-service users, organization by length of service, court referral versus self-referral, repeat listings of the same name, listings by family members. List the biases and how you will be able to correct for them or will need to include them in a discussion of your sample's limitations.

8) What specific type of probability sample will you choose (simple random, systematic)? Include your rationale and consider stratification prior to systematic sampling as a means of enhancing the representativeness of your sample. For stratification, on what variable(s) (sample member characteristics) would you stratify and why?

9) Indicate the specific procedure for asking people to participate. Indicate who will screen potential sample members and how they will do it.

10) When you ask people to participate, some will refuse. You should keep a tally of how many refuse so that you can calculate and report a participation rate. Also, it is helpful later, when considering possible biases of your sample, to compare participants with those who refused to participate. What information could you collect about nonparticipants (from observation, screening questions) that would enable you to make comparisons?

11) What size will your sample be? Indicate your rationale and discuss the feasibility of your sample size relative to time; expense; means of contact; and level of difficulty in contact, screening, and selection.

12) Pay close attention to the inclusion and representation of racial and ethnic groups in your study population. Racial and ethnic groups are frequently underrepresented in research studies. If a group comprises a small percentage of your study population, then any sample will likely result in too few persons to provide enough information to analyze. In that situation, oversample the underrepresented group if possible. You can consult a research text or a researcher to learn how to oversample and how to weight your data to take this into account. Do *not* report results where you pool racial or ethnic groups into a category labeled "other." It is disrespectful and provides no useful information.

Indicate steps you will take to ensure that racial and ethnic groups will be included in your sample in sufficient numbers to provide meaningful data about them.

13) In summary, state clearly to whom you expect to be able to generalize your findings, based on the sampling plan you have devised.

14) Summarize the strengths and limitations of your sample design—for example, the type of sample and its weaknesses, the size of your sample, and its generalizability.

B. FOR NONPROBABILITY SAMPLES

1) What is your specific group of interest?

2) What are the possible sources that you have considered for obtaining sample members and the pros and cons of each?

3) What are the screening and selection criteria for your sample?

Example: 1) at least 18 years of age, 2) with at least one child, and 3) a first time recipient of services at the agency. Be sure to specify the time frame (e.g., within the month of March). Indicate the specific procedure for sample selection.

4) You will probably need to explore your sample selection with your field instructor. In some instances you might need to know confidential information about people (diagnoses, problem situations) in order to determine their potential inclusion in your sample—for example, a study of teens identified as alcohol or drug abusers in a child welfare agency that serves all categories of children. Generally in those situations, agency personnel must first obtain client permission before releasing names to you, even though you are in placement at the agency. This is especially true in large agencies that have several divisions.

Sometimes this ethical consideration is disregarded, and it is your responsibility as an ethical researcher to ensure attention to it. To help you consider how important it is to have client consent for release, consider how you would feel if someone was giving to others that particular information about you or one of your children.

Indicate any planned safeguards for obtaining confidential information.

5) What specific type of sample will you draw?

6) Indicate the specific procedure for asking people to participate. Indicate who will screen potential sample members and how they will do it.

7) When you ask people to participate, some will refuse. You should keep a tally of how many refuse so that you can calculate and report a participation rate. Also, it is helpful later, when considering possible biases of your sample, to compare participants with those who refused to participate. What information could you collect about nonparticipants (from observation, screening questions) that would enable you to make comparisons?

8) What size will your sample be? Indicate your rationale and discuss the feasibility of your sample size relative to time; expense; means of contact; and level of difficulty in contact, screening, and selection.

9) Pay close attention to the inclusion and representation of racial and ethnic groups in your study population. Racial and ethnic groups are frequently underrepresented in research studies. If a group comprises a small percentage of your study population, then any sample will likely result in too few persons to provide enough information to analyze. Do **not** report results where you pool racial or ethnic groups into a category labeled "other." It is disrespectful and provides no useful information.

Indicate steps you will take to ensure that racial and ethnic groups will be included in your sample in sufficient numbers to provide meaningful data about them. Because experiences vary across cultures, how will you ensure that your study will reflect those differences?

10) Summarize the strengths and limitations of your sample design.

C. WRITE THE SAMPLE SECTION

This first draft should be approximately two pages and cover the details of your sampling design. Later, after you have collected your data, you will add how your sampling procedures actually occurred, including participation rate and the demographic characteristics of your sample members.

If possible, compare participants to nonparticipants on any information you may have for both groups (age, race, gender, or social class) to provide information about the extent to which participants are similar to, or different from, nonparticipants.

CHAPTER 11

PROTECTION OF RESEARCH PARTICIPANTS

REMINDER:
> Review your text on the protection of research participants and constructing consent forms.

Earlier you determined the procedures of the university and agency for protecting research participants and obtaining approval of research studies. Review boards typically require information about the proposed data collection procedures, sample selection, and informed consent, as well as copies of data collection instruments (including the interview agenda for qualitative studies). You have developed this information in earlier chapters of the workbook. Now you will complete the following sections, putting the information into the required format.

Research participants must be provided with information about the study and how it might affect them. A parent or guardian can act on behalf of participants who cannot understand or consent for themselves. With few exceptions, parental consent is required for participants who are under age 18.

When using innocuous and anonymous questionnaires in survey research, a consent form is usually not required; however, you have an ethical obligation to provide information about the study to the participants. This is usually done in a cover letter accompanying a mailed survey or verbally in the instructions given to a group of participants. Check with your university's IRB for clarification.

Social workers have additional obligations relative to the ethical conduct of research. If, based on participant responses, you become aware that someone is being abused or might harm himself or herself or another person, you are obligated to report it to the appropriate agency or authority. If you anticipate situations where this might be revealed, you should include in your consent form that you have a legal responsibility to report these incidents and would be obligated to violate the participant's confidentiality relative to that issue.

A. OUTLINE PROCEDURES FOR OBTAINING INFORMED CONSENT

Please note that young children are usually asked orally for their assent to participate in a study. If young children are participating in your study, indicate how you will obtain assent from them. Include the script you will use for obtaining assent. For older children and teens, many IRBs require a written assent form, similar to the consent form which must be signed by parents or legal guardians, in order for people under age 18 to participate in your study. Again, check with your IRB.

Indicate how you plan to inform participants about the study and obtain their consent to participate. Include specific procedures for children or youth under age 18 if applicable and their guardians.

B. CONFIDENTIALITY SAFEGUARDS

1) Describe how you will protect the privacy and confidentiality of the research participants at the time you collect the data.

2) Describe your plans for storage and protection of data, including the signed consent forms. *Do not take this instruction lightly.* We have all seen media stories about people whose laptops containing confidential data were stolen from their cars. Copies of surveys or interview notes can also be stolen from your vehicle; backpacks containing those items can be stolen; memory sticks with confidential data can be left at a public computer. Protect confidential data as you would have others protect yours. This should include, at a minimum password protection of all computer files and securing hard copies in locked file cabinets. Also, indicate a date at which point your data will be deleted or destroyed. We recommend you include this information in your consent form.

3) Describe your plans for protecting privacy and confidentiality in your presentation of findings and written report.

C. CONSTRUCT A CONSENT FORM

REMINDER:
IRB and agency approval must be obtained before collecting data.

Use the guidelines provided by the university IRB for what to include in the consent form. Although we have included samples of consent forms at the end of this chapter, be sure to check with your university's IRB. We recommend that you also ask for sample consent forms from the university IRB or your course instructor. Your methods text will also give information about constructing consent forms. You will submit the consent form along with your packet of information to the IRB.

A note regarding online surveys: since a signed consent form is not possible electronically, you need to specify exactly how you will fully inform and gain consent from your participants. Generally, you will include the information required for a traditional consent form prior to the actual survey instrument. With online surveys as with some methods of administering a survey, it is impossible to ensure complete anonymity, so you need to discuss how you will maintain confidentiality. Also, provide specific information about who to contact for questions about the study. Finally, participants will need to confirm a statement that they understand the purpose of the study, the potential risks, and their right to skip any questions, to withdraw from the study at any time, or to not participate at all. This can be done by having participants check an "I agree" box in order to continue with the survey.

1) List the points or items you must include in your consent form according to the

university IRB and agency requirements.

2) Next, prepare a draft of the consent form. Obtain feedback from your course instructor and agency instructor. Revise and finalize the consent form.

D.   REQUEST AGENCY APPROVAL

Indicate the steps you have taken for agency approval of your study. The agency may or may not have a specific process for approval of research. If there is no agency process in place, we encourage you to obtain written permission to carry out the study from the director of the agency. Submit a copy of your university IRB application packet with your request.

E.   REQUEST IRB APPROVAL

Using your drafts, prepare the IRB application packet for the university and any additional information required by the agency IRB.

SAMPLE INFORMED CONSENT FORM

We would like you to participate in the Evaluation of *[program name]*. Your participation is important to us and will help us assess the effectiveness of the program. As a participant in *[program name]* we will ask you to *[complete a questionnaire, answer questions in an interview, or other task]*.

We will keep all of your answers confidential. Your name will never be included in any reports and none of your answers will be linked to you in any way. The information that you provide will be combined with information from everyone else participating in the study.

[If information/data collection includes questions relevant to behaviors such as child abuse, drug abuse, or suicidal behaviors, the program should make clear its potential legal obligation to report this information—and that confidentiality may be broken in these cases. Make sure that you know what your legal reporting requirements are before you begin your evaluation.]

You do not have to participate in the evaluation. Even if you agree to participate now, you may stop participating at any time or refuse to answer any question. Refusing to be part of the evaluation will not affect your participation or the services you receive in *[program name]*.

If you have any questions about the study you may call *[name and telephone number of evaluator, program manager, or community advocate]*.

By signing below, you confirm that this form has been explained to you and that you understand it.

Please Check One:
- ❑ AGREE TO PARTICIPATE
- ❑ DO NOT AGREE TO PARTICIPATE

_____
Signed
Participant or Parent/Guardian

_____
Date

From: United State Department of Health and Human Services. (1997). *The Program Manager's Guide to Evaluation, p. 77.*

NOTE: We recommend adding a statement about data safeguards and a date for when the project data will be deleted or destroyed.

INFORMED CONSENT TO PARTICIPATE IN A STUDY OF THE CRISIS PROGRAM AT HUCKLEBERRY HOUSE YOUTH SERVICES

1. **Why is the study being conducted?** Huckleberry House is conducting a study to find out if the agency's crisis program is helpful to families. You have been asked to take part because you have used these services.

2. **What are you being asked to do?** You will be one of about 25 youth who are interviewed about their experience with the program and program staff. You will be asked some questions about what brought you to the program and what problems you and your parent(s) have been experiencing. We will contact you three months from now to see if things have changed for you. The interview usually takes about 30 minutes. Your first interview will be on the premises of Huckleberry House. Your second interview in three months will be by telephone.

3. **Is this voluntary?** Yes. You are under no obligation to participate. If you agree to participate, you can ask the interviewer to skip any questions that you'd rather not answer. Also, you are free to stop the interview at any time. You are also free to decline to participate in the follow-up interview.

4. **What are the advantages of participating?** Participating in this study will help Huckleberry House improve its services to youth and their families.

5. **Will participating in this study affect the services you are receiving?** No. Whether or not you agree to participate in the study will not affect the type or amount of services you are eligible to receive.

6. **Is this confidential?** Yes. Nothing learned about you by the researchers will be told to anyone else. The study staff will remove identifying information from your completed questionnaire. All records will be identified only by a number, and the link between that number and your name will be kept in a locked file that is available only to the researchers, not to Huckleberry House program staff. Once the study is completed, all records of your name will be destroyed. All data will be kept in locked files. Everything that you say is strictly confidential, and any reports or other published data based on this study will appear only in the form of summary statistics without names or other identifying information.

7. **What risks do you face if you participate?** There are no risks expected if you answer the questions.

8. **Who do you contact if you have questions about this research?** If you have any questions about the study, you can ask your interviewer or call the agency director, _____, at _____ or the faculty supervisor of this project, _____ at _____.

Your signature below indicates that you consent to be interviewed, that you have been given a copy of this consent form, and that you have read and understood it.

Signature:_____ Date: _____

Witnessed by:

Signature:_____ Date: _____

CHAPTER 12

DATA ANALYSIS FOR SURVEYS AND OUTCOME EVALUATIONS

This chapter of the workbook provides information on how to present the data you have collected and how to statistically analyze it. In this chapter, we introduce only the most commonly used bivariate statistical tests: chi-square (from cross tabulation tables), t-test (two groups), ANOVA (for multiple groups), and correlation (for two continuous variables). Our presentation of the bivariate tests assumes you have had prior instruction and understand which tests are appropriate to use. Remember that bivariate analyses are only suggestive of relationships, not definitive—multivariate analyses may reveal more complex relationships among several variables. For more complex analyses or those involving sample sizes less than 20, we recommend that you consult other sources. We suggest Weinbach and Grinnell's (2006) *Statistics for Social Workers* or Green and Salkind's (2007) *Using SPSS for Windows* for helpful information on statistical analysis.

The chapter is divided into five sections: (A) presentation of descriptive information, (B) presentation of group comparisons, (C) statistical tests for univariate data, (D) statistical tests for group comparisons, and (E) consideration of moderating variables. The data analysis we cover here is similar for survey methods and outcome evaluations, as well as existing data collected previously by others.

A WORD FOR THE STATISTICALLY INTIMIDATED

Many people are intimidated by statistics. Too often they believe that "only people who are good in math can understand statistics." This belief leads them to assume they cannot do any analysis involving statistics. This is simply not true. If you consider yourself statistically challenged, in this chapter we will show you that you can do basic, useful statistical analyses for your study.

At one level statistics are simply information. *In this study, 47 people were enrolled in the intervention. Of all study participants, 39% completed it successfully. The mean age of males was 22.3, compared to the mean years of females at 20.6.* Those are statistics.

There are other, less intuitive statistics as well, and this is what often throws people into a tizzy. *The correlation between number of sessions completed and score on the locus of control scale was .43. The effect size of an intervention designed to reduce recidivism among* *juvenile offenders was 1.2. In a logistic regression model of aggression among males, after controlling for race and age, the only statistically significant predictor was exposure to violence in the home—the odds ratio was .76, p <.05.* Already some of you may feel a headache coming on.

You may not be able to complete a particular statistical analysis on your own. Or even understand what it says without help. That's okay. You can find someone with more training than you who can help—much as you might consult with a social worker with more training than you on how to handle a difficult client situation. In both instances the important skill is knowing the right questions to ask—critical thinking.

How much of an effect did this intervention have, based on some standardized agreement about how to measure effects across different studies using different measures? Is a 10% difference between males and females on gains in functioning all that significant? To answer those questions you need both critical thinking skills and statistical knowledge. You have to rely on yourself for the former. For the latter don't hesitate to consult with others and add to your knowledge base.

COMPUTER ANALYSIS

Your first task is to organize the data you have collected. You will have to decide whether you will do hand tabulation or computer data entry and analysis. The advantages of the latter should be obvious, but you may have a small sample and plan to provide only basic tables and descriptive statistics, in which case statistical software, while expedient, would not be necessary.

Any number of statistical programs are available, including programs for advanced statistical analysis—such as SPSS and SAS. These are not difficult to learn but do require some effort. Spreadsheet programs you may already know—such as Excel—also allow for basic statistical analysis. There are a variety of texts available using these programs; we don't discuss them here. We believe that, unless you often collect and analyze data or you plan to do data analysis for a living, your time is better spent learning the *logic* of data analysis. If you really want to learn how to drive, take a course; otherwise, hire a cab. Just be sure you know where you want to go.

DESCRIPTIVE VS. INFERENTIAL STATISTICS

Statistical measures fall into two broad categories: descriptive and inferential. *Descriptive statistics* do just that: describe a sample and relationships among variables in the sample. For example, looking at Table 1 on page 146, you will find statistics about the rates of return for HIV test results for three different racial groups. In Table 2 you will find statistics about the percentage of persons who attended all their classes and the average number of incidents by two different groups. These statistics describe the sample.

Inferential statistics are measures that people use in an attempt to infer something *beyond* their sample. To what extent do the sample findings represent what is true in the larger population from which they drew their sample? For example, based on the data in Table 1, can we say that, among all clinic patients we drew our sample from, patients who are African American are less likely to return for their HIV test results than patients who are White or Hispanic? To answer that we use a chi-square statistic, noted at the bottom of the table. Anytime we want to generalize from our sample to the larger population from which we drew the sample, we need to use inferential statistics.

First, we discuss ways to present sample data and common measures employed to describe a sample. Then we take up inferential statistics.

TABLE CONSTRUCTION

Keep in mind that there are different formats for the presentation of your results. The APA Style Manual provides guidance for constructing and presenting tables in a manuscript. You can also look through the articles you used for your literature review for help with designing tables. However, tables presented in the literature may not follow APA formats. Check with your instructor regarding the required format. The key is to present your findings simply and clearly so they are easy to understand. We recommend that you have someone review your tables for clarity.

A. PRESENTATION OF DESCRIPTIVE INFORMATION

For the steps below, begin by drafting tables for your variables. Do not put values in the tables yet. As you work through the steps, you will develop several ideas about the best way to present your data and how you want your final tables to look. When you have decided the best format, then complete the tables with the data findings.

  1) Frequency Distributions:

  The most basic level of analysis involves calculating how many people gave a certain response to each question and in what categories. This information is referred to as a frequency distribution. You may group some categories of responses together rather than report a long series of responses. For example, rather than report how many people were of every age between 20 and 89, you can group categories together into intervals such as 20-29, 30-39, etc. Then, report the number of participants in each grouped interval. Consult a text for assistance in constructing intervals.

  For continuous variables you may also report, or only report, the means of variables and other associated statistics that will be discussed in the next section. You may choose to display some of your findings in graph form (bar, line, or pie chart). Make your choices based on what makes the presentation of findings easiest for your audience to understand. Refer to a research text for how to construct various graphs.

  On a separate sheet, list all of the variables in your study. Mark those variables that you think would be best presented with a graph (bar, line, or pie chart) in addition to or instead of a table. Sketch the types of graphs you plan to use.

  2) Means, Medians, and Standard Deviations:

  Reporting the *mean* (commonly referred to as the average) requires that the variables are continuous (such as age and income) rather than discrete (e.g., gender, race, and religion).

You will be interested in knowing the mean of all the responses to a particular question (e.g., the average age of the participants in your study). Knowing the *median* (middle) value of the variables is also informative, especially when there are extremely high or low scores, which will create a skewed mean.

If you are using a computer for data analysis, you can also easily calculate and report the standard deviations for your continuous variables. Remember, the *standard deviation* shows the dispersion of the data—how the scores are distributed around the mean. A high standard deviation alerts us that there is a large amount of variation among individual scores in the sample. It is most helpful when comparing two groups. For example, we might be interested in comparing the number of sessions attended by teens in two different types of treatment. A comparison of the standard deviations would tell us which group had more variation in attendance.

In your list of study variables determine those that are continuous and calculate the mean, median, and standard deviation.

3) Order of Presentation:
Decide which descriptive statistics to present in your report and the order in which you will present them. Often, more than one table is helpful. For example, one table may present the demographic characteristics of the sample and another may present frequencies of the key variables in your study. Begin with general information and move to specific findings that answer your research question. Again, we encourage you to look at how data were presented in other articles.

To help organize your presentation of descriptive findings make two lists: primary findings and secondary findings. The primary findings should relate directly to your research question and should be given the most attention in your narrative and visual presentations.

Organize your primary and secondary findings, sketching out mock tables and graphs. Then complete the tables with the results from your sample.

B. PRESENTATION OF GROUP COMPARISONS

Commonly, we are interested in comparing different groups of people on certain characteristics. Group comparisons are bivariate (two variable) analyses. They are used to provide additional information about the sample separated into groups. For example, in a needs assessment, you may be interested in comparing the identified needs (variable 1) reported by men versus women (variable 2). Or you might want to compare the number of sessions attended (variable 1) for two different groups of participants—self-referred individuals and court-referred individuals (variable 2). Group comparisons provide that information.

Table 1 shows an example of how descriptive data might be broken down by racial group and presented for a sample of clients who were tested for HIV at a clinic. (The inferential statistics at the bottom of the tables are discussed in the next section.)

Table 1

Returned for HIV Test Results and HIV Risk Level by Racial Group

	Racial Group		
	African American n = 63	Hispanic n = 14	White n = 121
Returned for HIV test result [a]	76.2% (48)	85.7% (12)	93.4% (113)
Risk level [b] (1-low to 10-high)			
Mean	2.0	2.5	3.3
Standard Deviation	2.7	4.4	6.3
Median	2	2	3

[a] Chi-Square = 11.1, p = .004 Cramer's V = .24
[b] F (ANOVA) = 1.27, p = .282

Note: The fact that Table 1 presents data for only three racial groups is, unfortunately, characteristic of much research. When the number of persons in a racial or ethnic group is small, they are either excluded from the analysis or worse, lumped into a category labeled "Other," which is of little value. This is why we suggest in the chapter on sampling that people make an effort to include sufficient numbers of persons in the various racial or ethnic groups that comprise their study population.

If your data do not include a sufficient number of persons within two or more racial or ethnic groups, *do not* combine them into a category called "Other." Recognize it as a limitation of your study and commit to drawing a better sample next time.

Table 2 provides an example of comparing participants on two different outcomes (attended all classes and number of incidents) in two programs, a Therapeutic Arts Program and a Recreational Program.

Table 2
Attended all Classes and Number of Incidents by Group Assignment

| | Groups | |
	Therapeutic Arts Program n = 22	Recreational Program n = 26
Attended all classes	68% (15)	73% (19)
Number of incidents		
Mean	4.0	4.2
Standard Deviation	5.5	4.5
Median	3	3

[a] Chi-Square = .138, p = .71 phi = .054
[b] t = -.107, p = .916 Effect size = -.04

1) List on a separate page in columns the groups you would like to compare. In rows to the left of the columns list the variables on which you would like to compare the groups.

2) Calculate the number of persons in each category.

3) For each group, calculate the descriptive statistics—for example, the frequency, mean, standard deviation, median, or percentage and number—of the responses to each variable of interest. Enter them in the appropriate cells in tables on a separate sheet.

   We provide mock tables on the next page as models for you to use. Although these represent program outcomes, they can be used for any group comparisons (male versus female, service users versus non-users, etc.).

   Be sure to include the sample size, group size, and group percentages for comparison purposes.

The following table shows how to present data for two groups compared on a dichotomous measure (a measure with only two categories) at one point in time—for example, at posttest for a treatment and control or comparison group.

Table number

Table name

	Groups	
	Treatment Group (n)	Control or Comparison Group (n)
Achieved	% (n)	% (n)
Not Achieved	% (n)	% (n)

$\chi^2 =$, p = , phi or Cramer's V =

The following table shows how you can present data for two groups compared on a continuous measure—for example, pretest and posttest measures for a treatment group and a comparison group.

Table number

Table name

	Groups	
	Treatment Group (n)	Control or Comparison Group (n)
Measure at Pretest Mean Standard Deviation	(n)	(n)
Measure at Posttest Mean Standard Deviation	(n)	(n)

t = , p = , Effect size =

STATISTICAL SIGNIFICANCE

Bivariate and multivariate analyses use various statistical tests, each designed to answer the same question: How likely is it that these results are a function of chance? When we say the results are statistically significant, we are saying that our findings are not likely to be just a fluke. We are willing to conclude that our observations in the sample can be generalized to the population we studied.

For example, looking at Table 1, our findings show that a higher percentage of Whites return to the Kansas City Free Health Clinic for their HIV test results than do African Americans or Hispanics. Is this a finding that we can attribute to the relationship between race and returning for results? Or is it merely due to chance and not likely to be found in another sample of HIV testers? If we find statistical significance, we conclude that our finding is probably *not* due to chance, and we may decide to develop an intervention to increase the rate at which African Americans and Hispanics return for their HIV test results.

Statistical testing, then, allows us to minimize chance as a possible explanation for the result we found. Sampling error plays a key role in statistical testing. To the extent that your sample is "off" in its representation of the study population, you introduce *chance* as an alternative explanation for anything you find.

This is why researchers emphasize using strong sample designs. Probability sampling, an assumption for many statistical tests, is a process of systematically and precisely selecting a group of people from a population in such a way as to best represent the population. How well was that accomplished? With statistical testing you can calculate a measure of how much error there is in using the sample's findings to generalize to the population. That's where sampling error (or margin of error) comes into play.

In conducting a statistical test you are actually converting your findings into a standardized value that results in a test statistic (e.g., $t = 2.3$). That standardized value is then used to determine the probability (p-value) that the findings are due to chance. If the probability is too high that the findings may be a result of chance, you cannot generalize the findings to the population.

Computer analysis gives you the test statistic and the p-value that is associated with it. The p-value is what you are interested in. A low probability (low p-value, usually .05 or less) means that getting this finding by chance is low. We can conclude that our sample finding most likely (not definitively as there are no certainties in behavioral research) reflects what is actually happening in the study population. In other words, we can be confident in generalizing our findings to the larger population.

In Table 1 the probability of getting the differences among the three racial groups simply by chance, was quite low, $p = .004$. Therefore, we can generalize the findings from our sample to the population of all clients at the clinic, our study population (*not* to all people in the U.S. population). Five percent (.05) or less is generally accepted as the standard in social science research, but you will sometimes see .01 specified, or in cases of small samples, .10.

This is the key to understanding statistical analysis. Remember: *all statistical tests are tests of the probability that the findings can be attributed to chance.* If it's less than .05 (or .10 or .01—the choice should be specified before the statistic is computed), you know chance as a possible explanation for the finding can be tossed out the door. Sure, it's still a possibility, but at least a small one. (Some other possible explanations for your findings remain—measurement error, errors in data collection— and you should have already addressed those limitations to the best of your ability.)

Our responsibility is to reduce the chance of error as much as possible. We do that in three ways: adhering to research conventions (like standard p-values when analyzing quantitative data), increasing sample size whenever possible, and replication (efforts to duplicate previous findings).

THE IMPACT OF SAMPLE SIZE ON STATISTICAL POWER

You should understand the impact of sample size as you assess study findings. The larger your sample, the easier it is to rule out chance as a possible explanation for your findings. The larger the sample, the more of the population you are capturing, and the less room for a chance variation from the population. Hence, in large samples you have a greater chance of finding statistical significance (low p-values) and concluding that your finding represents what one would find happening in the entire study population. You could be wrong of course (Type I error), but researchers keep that likelihood small.

Conversely, the smaller the sample size, the harder it is to rule out chance as a possible explanation for your findings. The smaller the sample, the greater the risk that it may not represent the population well and the greater the risk that what you find may be peculiar to that sample, not the overall population.

Hence, in small samples sometimes it can be difficult to show statistically significant results. You may find p-values close to, but above, .05 and .10. This happens often in social work research because many of our study samples are often small. You won't read about it very often, however, because most journals are loathe to publish studies where the researchers were unable to rule out chance as an explanation at least 95% of the time.

Keep this in mind as you interpret your results. You may not have statistically significant results because your sample size is too small to rule out chance even when your results did reflect what was happening in the population (a Type II error). With p-values above the stated levels, you will have to conclude that you could not rule out chance as an explanation for your findings. You might be wrong of course, but the "next" study will have to demonstrate that.

Increasing one's sample size is not always an option, but you can at least conduct a *power analysis* to determine how easily or how difficult it would be to reach statistical significance given your sample size. A power analysis is essentially a calculation of the probability of being able to identify a relationship or group difference if there is one. It is a measure that, if calculated, is more often reported in the text of an article rather than within a table.

The power of a specific statistical test is not often calculated (or more generously stated, not often reported) in social work research for the likely reason that most research with small samples would not pass muster; that is to say, the power of our statistical analyses would be unacceptably small—most of us wouldn't be able to rule out chance as a possible explanation for our results if our lives depended on it. Fortunately they don't. Allen Rubin (2008) states it more eloquently.

It's mind-boggling to imagine that many researchers are implementing studies without taking statistical power analysis into account; consequently, they don't know the odds that they're spinning their wheels trying to confirm hypotheses that, even if true, have a low probability of being supported (p.528).

Calculating the power of a statistical test is not easy (although more and more statistical software is being developed with that capability) and may be beyond your capacity, but you should at least be aware that the smaller your sample size, the weaker your ability to find statistical significance. How small? No one likes to give a number on this because it varies from test to test and in relation to other factors (such as how many variables you are considering at one time), but we'll stick our necks out and say that sample sizes under 50 are going to need to show some fairly sizeable differences in group comparisons to demonstrate statistical significance. Does that mean that studies with samples less than 50 are a waste of time? By no means. But it's important to understand that the findings from such small samples require even more replication to support them.

EFFECT SIZES

Something else to keep in mind: statistically significant findings generally give no indication about the strength of a relationship. A person can draw such a large sample (e.g., by drawing on city or state vital statistics databases) that even the smallest differences or weakest relationships will test as statistically significant, because there's little room for error. That does not provide any information about the strength or size of the discovered relationship.

Effect size statistics provide a standardized measure of association, allowing you to determine, on a standard everyone holds in common, just how big the difference is that you found between groups in your study (for example, sex offender recidivism rates for states requiring colored license plates for previously convicted offenders versus states without such laws), or how strong the relationship is between characteristics you collected data on (e.g., number of sessions attended and final outcome).

Another advantage of using and reporting effect sizes is that they allow for comparisons across studies, regardless of specific outcomes or measurement instruments. As such, effect sizes form the basis for *meta-analyses*—finding the average effect size among several related studies.

There are two groups of effect size measures that are commonly used, and the irony of the standardizing process of an effect size measure is that there is no standardization in how people refer to the measures: effect size or measure of association.

Effect size measures are a lot like power analyses: rarely computed and rarely reported. We mention them to emphasize that a statistically significant finding suggests nothing about the strength of the relationship or the size of the treatment effect (with the exception of the Pearson r statistic).

A Brief Summary of the Statistical Testing Process

1) Choose a statistical test (e.g., Chi-square, t-test, ANOVA, correlation) and analyze the data
2) Examine the findings: If $p >$ preset level (.01, .05, .10), chance may explain the findings
3) Consider other explanations for the findings
   a) Measurement bias or error
   b) Data collection bias or error
   c) Sampling error
4) Evaluate the power of the statistical tests to detect statistical significance (should be $>.80$)
5) Determine the strength or effect size of the significant relationships

C. STATISTICAL TESTS FOR UNIVARIATE DATA

1) Make a list of the descriptive findings you want to generalize to the population (e.g., mean, median, and standard deviation for age, percent using services, percent following through with a referral, mean number of sessions attended). Indicate whether each variable is continuous or discrete.

2) Using a statistical program, you might also construct a 95% confidence interval around the sample estimate. For continuous variables you will use the standard error of the mean. For discrete variables you will use the margin of error.

3) Create the table you will use to present these data. In many cases you will simply add this information to the tables you created in Section A.

D.   STATISTICAL TESTS FOR GROUP COMPARISONS

If your design is a one group pretest-posttest design, go to Part 1, otherwise skip to Part 2.

1) For one group pretest-posttest design:

a) When the outcome measure is discrete:

While similar to a cross tabulation, in this instance there is no grouping variable since there is only one group. The two variables are the dichotomous (yes or no) measures at pretest and posttest. Use the following table as a model to present your outcome results. Include the McNemar significance test (one of the nonparametric tests). Look for examples in your empirical articles.

Table number
Table name

	Time	
	Pretest	Posttest
	(n)	(n)
Achieved	% (n)	% (n)
Not Achieved	% (n)	% (n)

McNemar =   , p =   , phi or Cramer's V =

b) When the outcome measure is continuous (one group pretest-posttest design):

To statistically examine the change for participants from baseline (when pretest measures were taken) to the end of the intervention (when posttest measures are taken) *in one group,* you must conduct a dependent groups t-test (also referred to as a correlated groups t-test, a paired groups t-test, or matched groups t-test). This allows you to determine whether any change in the outcome measure from pre- to posttest is big enough to suggest the change was not due to chance.

Complete the following table.

Table number
Table name

	Outcome Measure
Pretest	(n)
Mean	
Standard Deviation	
Posttest	(n)
Mean	
Standard Deviation	

t =   , p =

2) For comparison or control group designs, refer to the tables you developed in Section B and add the appropriate statistical measures:

a) When the outcome measure is discrete: Conduct a chi-square statistical test of the differences between the two groups.

b) When the outcome measure is continuous: Conduct an independent groups t-test of the differences between the two group means.

E. TESTING THE RELATIONSHIP BETWEEN CONTINUOUS VARIABLES

In some instances, you may wish to compare two variables that are both continuous. For example, in an HIV clinic study, the staff members were interested in how a person's self-appraisal of HIV risk was related to (1) the number of sexual partners he or she had indicated and (2) the person's age. Using a Pearson correlation coefficient (r), they reported that risk increases with an increase in the number of sex partners. They did not find a statistically significant relationship between risk and age.

Table 3
Correlations between HIV Risk and Selected Characteristics

	HIV Risk (n=122)
Number of sex partners in past 12 months	$r = .28*$
Age	$r = .14$

*$p < .01$

Remember that the correlation measure (r) is also a measure of association, relationship strength, and effect size. In the above table the correlation between number of sex partners and risk is moderate.

Create a table to present your outcome results.

Table Number
Table Name

	Key Variable (n=)
Variable 1	$r =$
Variable 2	$r =$

*$p <$

F.   CONSIDERATION OF MODERATING VARIABLES

In some instances it will be helpful to consider moderating variables, those variables which might affect the relationships you have found when examining only two variables. For example, if we look again at Table 1 regarding return rates for HIV test results among racial groups, how might those results vary if we considered gender? In other words, could it be that gender accounts for differences in return rates rather than race? What would happen to our finding if we "controlled" for gender, that is, took gender into account? What about controlling for age differences? What about type of risk a person has for becoming HIV+?

As you can see, the list of other possible explanations for return rate—or whatever variable you are studying—can become long. We refer to this as the "black hole of research"—there is always the possibility that another variable exists that we have not yet identified that might change our findings. Consequently, some people analyze their data by considering every possible combination of variables and looking for any statistically significant results. And they are often referred to as "data miners." The danger of such an occupation is that based on probabilities, there will likely be at least one significant test result for every 20 tests that are run—the statistical equivalent of "fool's gold."

Theoretical purists would argue that theory or theoretical models should drive data analysis. In our example, prior to data collection, one might draw upon a Health Beliefs Model or Theory of Reasoned Action or the literature to develop hypotheses about what variables are related to HIV-testing behaviors.

In reality most people use a mix of both approaches—they have a map (theoretical models, previous studies, logic models) about what relationships they are interested in studying (generally the basis for deciding what data to collect), but they also explore the data afterwards for other relationships they had not considered.

Now back to your data. Consider other possible variables from among those you have collected. Consider those that would be worth controlling for, worth testing as moderating variables, because theoretically they are linked, they have been identified in prior studies, or your analyses so far suggest you may have missed some significant relationships. We provide a table template for presentation of three dichotomous variables, but you could have more than two categories; adjust as needed. If you have combinations of categorical and continuous variables you'd like to analyze for possible moderating effects, it's worth consulting with a data analyst because the analysis gets trickier.

Table number
Table name

Variable 3	Variable 1			
	Category A		Category B	
	Variable 2			
	Category A	Category B	Category A	Category B
Category A				
Category B				

Note: Chi-square statistic tests for a multi-layered table would be presented for two variables at a time.

CHAPTER 13

DATA ANALYSIS FOR QUALITATIVE RESEARCH

REMINDER:
> Review a text specifically devoted to qualitative methods. A general research text may not provide enough information for you to conduct a good qualitative analysis.

Recall that the goal of qualitative research is to provide an in-depth understanding of a phenomenon from the perspective of the research participants. Strategies for qualitative analysis vary and can be quite complicated. Keep in mind that you want to present the words and experiences of the research participants.

Your aim as a novice researcher is to conduct an analysis that organizes and summarizes the textual accounts of your participants and incorporates your observations. Your task is to identify themes and patterns in the data and offer interpretations of them. First, you will reduce the pages of text from your interviews, as well as any notes and observations that you have made, to a summary of common topics that participants have presented, with the goal of answering your research question. For each topic, you will identify and code excerpts from each participant, grouping similar topics together into categories. Second, you will examine all the excerpts in each code and compare and contrast them, identifying themes within each topic. Third, you will elaborate on and discuss the themes to answer your research questions and return to the literature to see how your findings compare to what others have said. Finally, you establish credibility by seeking feedback from the participants in your study. Because methods of qualitative analysis are less clear-cut than methods for quantitative analysis, another way to strengthen your study's findings is to specify as clearly and accurately as possible how you conducted the analysis.

We strongly suggest that you type or utilize voice recognition software to enter the text (either in its entirety or, at a minimum, the portions of the interviews that address your research topic) into a word processing program for analysis. Remember that there are software programs which can assist with qualitative analysis. These programs help *manage* the data, but you must be able to *do the interpretation* that is crucial to qualitative analysis. The steps we suggest for qualitative analysis do not require a specific software program. You will be able to conduct your analysis by using a word processing program to "cut and paste" your excerpts, moving them into topic files.

A. FIRST LEVEL CODING

1) Read through all the data—the interviews, your notes, and any other sources of data you have. As you read through your data several times, identify the common topics that participants discuss.

   Keep a list of all the topics you identify. Also, take notes (called analytical memos) of your thoughts and observations as you read the data. Read through the data until you cannot identify any new topics. List your topics on a separate page.

2) For each topic you have listed, identify the excerpts of text (often referred to as meaning units or content units) that relate to them by highlighting the relevant text. Excerpts are sections of each participant's responses that relate to each of your topics. Your task is to determine how much of the participant's comments are related to each topic. Your excerpts can range in length from a portion of a sentence to several paragraphs or pages, depending on how much the participant has said related
   to the topic.

   Here is where word processing software is invaluable. You can easily block, move, and copy excerpts into topic files.

3) Sort and organize the data by placing the excerpts into the topic areas you have identified. This step is commonly called *first level coding*. As you read, you will *constantly compare* each excerpt to the others. Excerpts with similar meanings will be placed in the same topic area and given the same code.

   Codes are basically short-hand notations for your topic areas. For example, if you are coding "participant responses related to positive interactions with social workers" you might assign a code POS SW to all the excerpts in which participants discuss that topic.

   Excerpts that are different will be assigned to different codes. Some excerpts may fit into more than one topic and therefore have more than one code.

4) Throughout the above process, reorder and refine your topics into categories of broader groupings of topics. You may identify new topics that you had not previously thought of. Add them to your list of categories.

B.   SECOND LEVEL CODING

Second level coding involves a deeper level of analysis and interpretation of the data. In first level coding, you placed similar excerpts from each participant together and assigned them a specific code. You also grouped the topic areas that related to each other into broader categories. In second level coding, you will look for patterns across the topics, commonly referred to as themes.

Now your task is to examine all excerpts with the same code to compare excerpts across individual participants. Read what all the participants said, all the excerpts, for each topic area. As you read, identify themes within the topic areas that are illustrated across the participants' responses.

1) On another sheet list your themes. Ask yourself:

   ✓ What are the main themes that are important to answering my research question?
   ✓ What similarities and differences do I see in the responses?
   ✓ Are there any relationships, trends, or patterns across responses?
   ✓ Are there exceptions to the themes I have identified?

2) Now arrange the themes you have identified to answer research questions.

   ✓ Which themes seem to belong together?
   ✓ What order of presentation of themes makes sense?

3) Be sure to include each participant's voice in your presentation. Select representative excerpts and anecdotal accounts for each theme. Provide one or two excerpts to include in the results section of your paper so that the reader can "see" how you arrive at your findings.

   On separate pages, compile the representative excerpts that you will include in your final paper.

C.   ELABORATE ON AND DISCUSS THEMES

1) Examine and provide your interpretation of the themes (findings) you have selected to answer your research question. Explain similarities and differences in, or exceptions to, the findings.

2) Finally, return to the literature to explore the concepts and ideas that emerged from your study. Identify themes and relationships that others have found and integrate them into the discussion section of your final report.

D.   ESTABLISH CREDIBILITY

An important step in qualitative research that will add credibility to your findings is to obtain feedback from your research participants regarding the categories, themes, trends, and patterns you identified. If possible, you may be able to reconvene a group or share a draft of your final report with some participants for their feedback on the findings of your study. Ask participants if they support or disagree with your findings and conclusions. Including their feedback in your final report will strengthen the credibility of your study.

Another way to establish credibility in your study is to carefully and thoroughly document what you have done and how you have done it. Include this information in the results section of your final report. It will clarify for the reader the choices you have made and why.

Indicate your plan to establish credibility in your study.

CAUTION:
You are reporting findings based on the people in your study only. You must be careful to avoid using findings to generalize to others. Rather, your study is exploratory and offers tentative suggestions that require further study. For a discussion of trustworthiness, credibility, dependability, and generalization, review a qualitative methods text.

CHAPTER 14

DATA ANALYSIS FOR SINGLE-CASE DESIGN RESEARCH

REMINDER:

Refer to a research text for ways to construct, analyze, and interpret graphed results of single-case design studies.

The significance of your single-case study findings should be evaluated in each of three ways: visual significance, statistical significance, and substantive (clinical) significance.

A. VISUAL SIGNIFICANCE

The first analysis, visual significance, is the primary way you use your study results with your client. The researcher-as-practitioner and the client share constant feedback during the intervention phase. You can review the results with the client by using the graphed data, allowing both of you to visualize the progress of your work together.

Visual significance is inherently a subjective assessment of your findings. Essentially, it asks you and the client to examine the graphed results and determine from your points of view whether the intervention was successful.

On a separate page draw a graph of your findings with the X- and Y-axes clearly marked, as well as all baseline and intervention phases. Connect the plotted points on the graph, and consider the visual significance of your findings.

1) What changes in the target goal do you observe? What is the trend at baseline and at intervention?

2) Comment on any abrupt or unusual changes that warrant explanation (e.g., if the number of temper tantrums spikes on a certain day, or if there are no temper tantrums on a certain day)?

3) Does it appear that the intervention was effective, ineffective, or unclear? Support your answer.

B. STATISTICAL SIGNIFICANCE

Sometimes the change or lack of change in outcome from baseline to intervention will be obvious, and a statistical analysis unnecessary. Other times it may be difficult to determine whether there is real change or a hopeful bias on your part. Determining statistical significance provides an objective method for evaluating your findings. It relies on the principles of probability theory to rule out chance fluctuations in your data as a possible explanation for your findings. This does not mean, however, that it eliminates the need for a thoughtful visual inspection of the data as outlined in the previous section.

Just as one should consider a statistically significant result in grouped data within the context of all the data analyzed, one should consider statistically significant single-case results within the context of the visual *picture* presented by the data. It is possible in both cases to have a statistically significant gain that is, in grouped data so small, or in single-case data so brief, that it represents no real change.

There are three procedures available for determining statistical significance in single-case studies. Refer to a text, and seek your instructor's assistance as you choose one of the following methods: celeration line, two standard deviation procedure, proportion/frequency procedure.

Complete one test, detailing how it was done and the final results.

C.   SUBSTANTIVE OR CLINICAL SIGNIFICANCE

The final analysis of the work done by two people (or more depending on the system studied) should not rest solely on final numbers. The numbers must be considered in a broader context. In assessing the clinical significance of this case, comment on the following questions:

- Do you and the client feel there has been substantial progress?
- Is the client functioning significantly better now than when you began your work together?
- Do the collateral persons in the client's life see a significant change?
- Is the change more, less, or equal to the change you've seen in other clients with similar situations?
- What have been your co-workers' experiences?
- How does the amount of change that occurred compare to the amount of time and effort it took—for both the client and the worker?
- How does it compare to the time and effort required when using other interventions?

Comment on the clinical significance of your findings. Also ask your client to comment on your work together and the graphed findings. Include your client's comments.

CHAPTER 15

WRITING THE FINAL REPORT

REMINDER:

Refer to the Research Paper Outline at the end of this chapter and to the APA publication manual.

This chapter focuses on presenting your findings in a written research paper. Basically, your report will include what you did and why, what you found, and what it means. Your research paper will expand on earlier chapters and include new sections on findings and discussion. From this paper, you can develop a presentation for your agency, for your peers in field placement, or for participants at a conference. If you are interested in submitting your study for publication, check with your course instructor for guidance.

Allow enough time to write your research report. Having completed each chapter of the workbook, you have a rough draft of your paper. We recommend that you follow the outline at the end of this chapter and write a second draft to share with your field instructor, agency staff, and peers for feedback and comments. You may also seek help from your school's writing center.

A. REVISE EARLIER SECTIONS

Revise earlier drafts of the Introduction and Literature Review sections, changing the tense from future (you will study) to past (you studied). Incorporate the feedback you received from your course instructor, field instructor, and others along the way.

B. REWRITE THE METHOD SECTION

1) Since studies do not usually proceed as initially planned, in your final Method section, specify how you carried out your study, including detail on exactly what you did and how you did it.

   ✓ Include your research design
   ✓ Present the measures that you used in your study
   ✓ Discuss the data collection procedures that you followed as you implemented your study

2) Revise your draft of Chapter 10 to include the results of your sampling procedures.

   ✓ Describe the criteria and procedures for sample selection as they were carried out in your study.
   ✓ Present the results of the sampling procedures, the response rate, and demographic characteristics of the sample members.
   ✓ Depending on how you selected your sample, compare participants to those who refused to participate

C. WRITE THE RESULTS SECTION

Organize and present the results, or findings, of your study.

1) In narrative form, present your primary and secondary findings.

2) Visually and textually display data that will help the reader understand your findings.

   ✓ When appropriate, display data in tables, graphs, or charts
   ✓ Write the narrative section to describe visual displays
   ✓ For qualitative studies, use excerpts identified in Chapter 12 to illustrate themes

3) Review the findings section of your report to be sure that you present the *results* of your study, not your interpretation of them.

D. WRITE THE DISCUSSION SECTION

Refer to the Research Paper Outline for the topics to be included. Use the following to develop a list of the main points to be included in this section. After you have made notes under each item, write the full draft of the discussion section.

1) Discuss your interpretation of the findings.

   ✓ Refer to your original research question and discuss what you learned about it.
   ✓ Refer to the literature you reviewed and comment on how your findings relate to that literature.

2) Develop implications for social work.

   What do the findings of your study mean for the agency, staff members, the participants, and/or the social work profession?

3) Provide recommendations for social workers.

   Based on your study, what policies, programs, and/or practice actions do you think should be taken by your agency or social work practitioners?

4) Summarize the previously-discussed limitations of your study relative to measures, data collection procedures, and sample design.

5) Make suggestions for future research.

   ✓ What else do we need to know that would help us better serve our clients?
   ✓ What would you recommend to the next researcher who wants to study this topic?
   ✓ What other questions evolved from this study? (Questions that emerged from your study that you think future research should address.)

E.   COMPILE THE REFERENCES AND APPENDICES

Include all the sources of information (journal articles, books, and reports) that you used in writing your report. Consult a style manual for proper form. In the Appendices include a copy of the consent form and your research instrument or interview agenda.

F.   WRITE THE ABSTRACT

An abstract is a brief overview summary of your study and results, usually 120 words or less. Write the abstract and place it immediately following your title page.

Following this page you will find two examples of an abstract written for the same study. The APA manual also provides guidance in writing your abstract.

G.   FINAL CHECKLIST

- ❑ Have you preserved the confidentiality of the research participants?
- ❑ Have you used gender-neutral language in your report?
- ❑ Have you properly cited work by other authors that you use in your report?
- ❑ Have you proofread your paper for grammar, punctuation, and spelling errors?
- ❑ Have you made sure that your paper is in the required format, usually APA for social work?

ABSTRACT EXAMPLE 1

Objectives: We sought to convey patient experiences with adherence to antiretroviral therapy and to develop recommendations for ways social workers can support adherence efforts.

Methods: We conducted three focus groups lasting two hours each with a total of 21 men, utilizing a semi-structured interview guide.

Results: Participants discussed their desire for information, the importance of the relationship with care providers, the impact of medication side effects, the role of social supports, and the responsibility of self as factors influencing adherence. Participants' discussion suggested a curvilinear relationship between adherence and severity of illness—adherence was more difficult when feeling fine or feeling terrible.

Conclusions: Social workers should educate themselves about antiretroviral regimens and side effects; help individuals gain access to information; facilitate relationships and enhance communication between patient and providers; start support groups or refer individuals to existing support groups; and provide greatest support for adherence when individuals are experiencing minimal or severe illness.

ABSTRACT EXAMPLE 2

People who are HIV positive and people who have been diagnosed with AIDS have new hope in the form of antiretroviral medications. However, many social workers remain unaware of the rigors of this treatment regimen and the difficulties it presents. This article presents the results of a qualitative study of HIV-positive individuals who have struggled with the adherence issues endemic to antiretroviral treatment and seeks to give voice to their experiences. In the process the article also seeks to educate social workers about antiretroviral treatment for HIV, the importance of adherence, and potential support strategies.

Research Paper Outline

Title Page

Abstract

Introduction
    Significance and purpose of study
    Relevance to social work
    Research question

Literature Review
    Background of the study
    Theories and concepts and variables
    Empirical studies
    Critical analysis and summary of literature
    Purpose and rationale for the study

Method
    Sample
        Selection of sample
        Characteristics of sample members
        Protections for research participants
    Procedures
        Research design
        Measures
        Data collection procedures

Results
    Narrative presentation
    Visual presentation: Tables, graphs, and charts

Discussion
    Interpretation of findings
    Implications and recommendations for social work
    Strengths and limitations of the study
    Suggestions for future research

References

Appendices
    Consent form
    Research instrument

BIBLIOGRAPHY

American Psychological Association. (2001). *Publication manual of the American Psychological Association* (5th ed.). Washington, DC.

Berg, B. L. (2007). *Qualitative research methods for the social sciences* (6th ed.). Boston, MA: Pearson, Allyn & Bacon.

Bloom, M., Fischer, J., & Orme, J. G. (2009). *Evaluating practice: Guidelines for the accountable professional* (6th ed.). Boston, MA: Allyn & Bacon.

Brophy, G. (2000). Social work treatment of sleep disturbance in a 5-year-old boy: A single-case evaluation. *Research on Social Work Practice, 10*(6), 749-760.

Dietz, T. J., Westerfelt, A., & Barton, T. R. (2004). Incorporating practice evaluation with the field practicum. *Journal of Baccalaureate Social Work, 9(*2), 78-90.

DiFranks, N. N. (2008). Social workers and the NASW Code of Ethics: Belief, behavior, disjuncture, *Social Work, (53)*2, 167-176.

Fischer, J., & Corcoran, K. J. (2006). *Measures for clinical practice: Vol. 1. Couples, families, children* (4th ed.). New York: Oxford University Press.

Fischer, J., & Corcoran, K. J. (2006). *Measures for clinical practice: Vol. 2. Adults* (4th ed.). New York: Oxford University Press.

Epstein, I. (1987). Pedagogy of the perturbed: Teaching research to the reluctants. *Journal of Teaching in Social Work, 1*(1), 71-89.

Forte, J. A., & Mathews, C. (1994). Potential employers' views of the ideal undergraduate social work curriculum. *Journal of Social Work Education, 30*(2), 228-240.

Gibbs, L. E. (2002). *Evidence-based practice for the helping professions: A practical guide with integrated multimedia.* Pacific Grove, CA: Wadsworth.

Ginsberg, L. H. (2001). *Social work evaluation: Principles and methods.* Needham Heights, MA: Allyn & Bacon.

Green, R. G., Bretzin, A., Leininger, C., & Stauffer, R. (2001). Research learning attributes of graduate students in social work, psychology, and business. *Journal of Social Work Education, 37*(2), 333-341.

Green, S. B., & Salkind, N. J. (2008). *Using SPSS for Windows and Macintosh: Analyzing and understanding data* (5th ed.). New York, NY: Pearson Prentice Hall.

Grinnell, R. M. (2008). *Social work research and evaluation: Quantitative and qualitative approaches* (8th ed.). New York, NY: Oxford Press.

Jordan, C., & Franklin, C. (2003). *Clinical assessment for social workers: Quantitative and qualitative methods* (2nd ed.). Chicago, IL: Lyceum.

Harrigan, M. P. & Koerin, B. B. (2007). Long-distance caregiving: Personal realities and practice implications. *Reflections:Narratives of Professional Helping, (13)*2, 5-16.

Kirk, S. A. (1990). Research utilization: The substruction of belief. In L. Videka-Sherman & W. J. Reid (Eds.), *Advances in Clinical Social Work Research.* Silver Spring, MD: National Association of Social Workers.

Kirk, S., & Fischer, J. (1976). Do social workers understand research? *Journal of Education for Social Work, 12,* 63-70.

Knight, C. (1993). A comparison of advanced standing and regular master's students' performance in the second-year field practicum: Field instructors' assessments. *Journal of Social Work Education, 29*(3), 309-317.

Leedy, P. D. & Ormron, J. E. (2005). *Practical research: Planning and design* (8th ed.). New York, NY: Pearson Prentice Hall.

Lincoln, Y. S., & Guba, E. G. (1985). *Naturalistic inquiry.* Beverly Hills, CA: Sage.

Marino, R., Green, R., & Young, E. (1998). Beyond the scientist-practitioner model's failure to thrive: Social workers' participation in agency-based research activities. *Social Work Research, 22*(3), 188-192.

Michalski, J. H., Mishna, F., Worthington, C., & Cummings, R. (2003). A multi-method impact evaluation of a therapeutic summer camp program, *Child and Adolescent Social Work Journal, (20)*1, 53-76.

Mokuau, N., Braun, K. L., Wong, L. K., Higuchi, P., & Gotay, C. C. (2008). Development of a family intervention for Native Hawaiian women with cancer: A pilot study. *Social Work (53)* 1, 9-19.

Montcalm, D. & Royse, D. (2002). *Data analysis for social workers.* Needham Heights, MA: Allyn & Bacon.

Mulroy, E. A. & Lauber, H. (2004). A user-friendly approach to program evaluation and effective community interventions for families at risk of homelessness, *Social Work, (49)*4, 573-586.

Neuman, W. L. (2004). *Basics of social research: Quantitative and qualitative approaches.* Needham Heights, MA: Allyn & Bacon.

Padgett, D. K. (2004). *The qualitative research experience.* Pacific Grove, CA: Wadsworth.

Patton, M. Q. (1990). *Qualitative evaluation methods.* Newbury Park, CA: Sage.

Riessman, C. K. (2008). Narrative Methods for the Human Sciences. Newbury Park, CA: Sage.

Rubin, A. (2008). Statistics for Evidence-Based Practice and Evaluation. Belmont, CA: Thompson Brooks/Cole.

Rubin, A., & Babbie, E. (2008). *Research methods for social work* (6th ed.). Belmont, CA: Thompson Brooks/Cole.

Siegel, D. H. (2003). Open adoption of infants: Adoptive parents' feelings seven years later. *Social Work 48*(3), 409-419.

United Way. (1996). *Measuring program outcomes: A practical approach.*

Weinbach, R. W. & Grinnell, R. M. (2007). Statistics for social workers (7th ed.). Boston, MA: Allyn & Bacon.

Yegidis, B. L., & Weinbach, R. W. (2009). *Research methods for social workers* (6th ed.). Boston, MA: Pearson Allyn & Bacon.